SPECTR

3A

A Communicative
Course in English

Diane Warshawsky
with Donald R. H. Byrd

Donald R. H. Byrd *Project Director*

Anna Veltfort *Art Director*

Longman

Library of Congress has cataloged the full edition of this title as follows:

Warshawsky, Diane.
    Spectrum 3, a communicative course in English / Diane Warshawsky
with Donald R. H. Byrd; Donald R. H. Byrd, project director; Anna
Veltfort, art director.
        p   cm.
Also published in a two-book split edition
ISBN 0-13-830068-2
    1. English language--Textbooks for foreign speakers.   I. Byrd,
Donald R. H. II. Title.
PE1128.W363 1994
428.3'4--dc20   93-26881
                                                              CIP

    ISBN (3A) 0-13-830076-3   ISBN (3B) 0-13-830118-2

Project Manager: Nancy L. Leonhardt
Manager of Development Services: Louisa B. Hellegers
Editorial Consultant and Contributing Writer: Larry Anger
Contributing Writer: Susan Stempleski
Development Editor: Stephanie I. Karras
Audio Development Editor: D. Andrew Gitzy
Assistants to the Editors: Sylvia P. Bloch, Adam Hellegers, Amy Adrion

Managing Editor: Sylvia Moore
Production Editors and Compositors: Jan Sivertsen, Christine McLaughlin Mann
Technical Support and Assistance: Molly Pike Riccardi, David Riccardi, Ken Liao
Production Coordinator: Ray Keating
Production Assistant: Ellen Gratkowski
Cover Design: Roberto de Vicq
Interior Concept and Page-by-Page Design: Anna Veltfort

Audio Program Producer: Paul Ruben

©1993 by Prentice Hall Regents
A Pearson Education Company
Pearson Education
10 Bank Street
White Plains, NY 10606

Printed in the United States of America

10 9 8 7

ISBN 0-13-830076-3

I N T R O D U C T I O N

Spectrum 3A and 3B represent the third level of a six-level course designed for adolescent and adult learners of English. The student book, workbook, and audio program for each level provide practice in all four communication skills, with a special focus on listening and speaking. Levels 1 and 2 are appropriate for beginning students and "false" beginners. Levels 3 and 4 are intended for intermediate classes, and 5 and 6 for advanced learners of English. The first four levels are offered in split editions — 1A, 1B, 2A, 2B, 3A, 3B, 4A, and 4B. The student books, workbooks, audio programs, and teacher's editions for levels 1 to 4 are also available in full editions.

Spectrum is a "communicative" course in English, based on the idea that communication is not merely an end-product of language study, but rather the very process through which a new language is acquired. *Spectrum* involves students in this process from the very beginning by providing them with useful, natural English along with opportunities to discuss topics of personal interest and to communicate their own thoughts, feelings, and ideas.

In *Spectrum*, comprehension is considered the starting point for communication. The student books thus emphasize the importance of comprehension, both as a useful skill and as a natural means of acquiring a language. Students begin each unit by listening to and reading conversations that provide rich input for language learning. Accompanying activities enhance comprehension and give stu-dents time to absorb new vocabulary and structures. Throughout the unit students encounter readings and dialogues containing structures and expressions not formally introduced until later units or levels. The goal is to provide students with a continuous stream of input that challenges their current knowledge of English, thereby allowing them to progress naturally to a higher level of competence.

Spectrum emphasizes interaction as another vital step in language acquisition. Interaction begins with simple communication tasks that motivate students to use the same structure a number of times as they exchange real information about themselves and other topics. This focused practice builds confidence and fluency and prepares students for more open-ended activities involving role playing, discussion, and prob-lem solving. These activities give students control of the interaction and enable them to develop strategies for expressing themselves and negotiating meaning in an English-speaking environment.

The *Spectrum* syllabus is organized around functions and structures practiced in thematic lessons. Both functions and structures are carefully graded according to level of difficulty, and usefulness. Structures are pre-sented in clear paradigms with informative usage notes. Thematic lessons provide interesting topics for interaction and a meaningful vehicle for introducing vocabulary.

Student Book 3A consists of seven units, each divided into one- and two-page lessons. Each unit begins with a preview page that outlines the functions/themes, language, and forms (grammar) in the unit. A preview activity prepares students to understand the cultural material in the conversations that begin each unit and gives them the opportunity to contribute their own background knowledge. The first lesson in each unit presents a series of realistic conversations, providing input for comprehension and language acquisition. New functions and structures are then practiced through interactive tasks in several thematic lessons. A one-page, fully illustrated comprehension lesson provides further input in the form of a dialogue and listening exercise both related to the storyline for the level. The next one-page lesson provides pronunciation practice and includes discussion or role-playing activities that draw on students' personal experience. The final lesson of the unit presents realistic documents such as historical texts and news articles for reading comprehension practice. Review lessons follow units 1 to 4 and units 5 to 7.

Workbook 3A is carefully coordinated with the student book. Workbook lessons provide listening and writing practice on the functions, structures, and vocabulary introduced in the corresponding student book lessons. Units end with a guided composition related to the theme of the reading in the student book.

Audio Program 3A offers two cassettes for the student book with all conversations, model dialogues, listening activities, and readings dramatized by professional actors in realistic recordings with music and sound effects. A third cassette includes the workbook listening activities.

Teacher's Edition 3A features full-sized color reproductions of each student-book page with teaching suggestions, listening scripts, and answer keys on the facing page. Listening scripts and answer keys for the workbook appear in the appendix.

A **Testing Package** includes a placement test as well as midterm and final tests for each level.

S C O P E A N D

S E Q U E N C E

PREVIEW

FUNCTIONS/THEMES	LANGUAGE	FORMS
Introduce someone	Have you met Marie? Yes, I have. Have you two met each other? No, I don't believe we have.	The present perfect: yes-no questions and short answers
Say how you know someone	We used to work together. We both teach at Kennedy High School. We're from the same hometown.	Formulaic use of *used to*
Say hello informally	How are you doing, Ted? Hi, Julia. Nice to see you.	
Talk about places you've been	Have you ever been to San Francisco? Yes, I've been there many times.	Past participles of some irregular verbs
Talk about things you've done	Have you ever gone snorkeling? No, I haven't. Have you? Yes, I have.	
Offer help Accept or decline help	Here, let me help you with that. Oh, thanks. That's very nice of you. That's O.K. I can manage.	Offers with *let*
Strike up a conversation	I hear you got a new job. Yes, I just started this week. I see you're reading *Time* magazine. I just got it this morning.	*Just* for the recent past
End a conversation	Enjoy yourself! It's been nice talking to you. I've enjoyed talking to you.	

Preview the conversations.

Where are the people in the pictures? Why are they there? Which people know each other? Which people don't know each other? What is happening in the second picture?

Imagine you are one of the people in the pictures. With two other classmates, act out the conversation.

1. Taking off

United Airlines Flight 856 is flying from Seattle, Washington, to Chicago, Illinois.

A

Laura Enders Jim Blake! What a surprise!

Jim Blake I don't believe it. What are you doing here in Seattle?

Laura Oh, I just spent a few days with my parents. Now I'm on my way back to Chicago.

Jim Gee, it's been a long time.

Laura It sure has. Say, I hear you started your own computer business.

Jim How did you know?

Laura My mother. She keeps track of all my old friends.

B

Monica Blake (*Coughs*)

Jim Oh, I'm sorry. Have you two met each other?

Laura No, I don't believe we have.

Jim Laura, this is my wife, Monica. Monica, I'd like you to meet Laura Enders. Laura and I went to high school together.

Monica It's nice to meet you, Laura.

Laura Nice to meet you, too.

Announcer (*Over loudspeaker*) United Airlines Flight 856 to Chicago is now boarding at Gate 9.

Laura Oh, that's my flight. I have to go.

Monica We've got a plane to catch, too.

Laura Where are you off to?

Monica We're taking a week off and going to Hawaii.

Laura Oh, really? Have you been there before?

Monica Yes, a few times.

Laura Well, enjoy yourselves.

Monica Thanks, we will.

Laura Great seeing you, Jim. Nice meeting you, Monica.

Jim Same here.

Monica and Jim Bye.

Doug Lee I see you're reading the new Stephen King novel. How do you like it?
Laura I can't put it down. Have you read it?
Doug Yes. As a matter of fact, I just finished it. The ending's great.
Laura Don't tell me! I'm almost done.
Doug Are you from Chicago?
Laura Well, I'm originally from Seattle, but I live in Chicago now.
Doug How do you like it?
Laura Very much. Have you ever been to Chicago before?
Doug No, I haven't. This is my first trip. I have a job interview there. By the way, my name's Doug Lee.
Laura I'm Laura Enders.

Flight attendant Here, let me help you get that down.
Laura Oh, thanks. That's very kind of you.
Doug Well, it's been nice talking to you, Laura.
Laura I've enjoyed talking to you, too, Doug. Good luck on your interview.
Doug Thanks. I really want this job.

Figure it out

1. Listen to the conversations. Then choose the correct answers.

1. Jim and Laura
   a. have known each other a long time.
   b. haven't known each other a long time.

2. Doug and Laura
   a. have known each other a long time.
   b. haven't known each other for very long.

2. Read the sentences. Listen to the conversations again and say *True* or *False*.

1. Laura lives in Seattle. *False.*
2. Jim and Laura are from the same hometown.
3. Laura and Monica have met before.
4. Doug has read the new Stephen King novel.
5. Doug has a job in Chicago.

3. Do the sentences in each pair have the same meaning or different meanings? Say *Same* or *Different*.

1. Where are you off to?
   Where are you going? *Same.*

2. I just finished it.
   I finished it a long time ago.

3. What are you doing here in Seattle?
   Why are you here in Seattle?

4. We're taking a few days off.
   We're not going to work for a few days.

5. Have you been to Chicago before?
   Are you from Chicago?

6. Have fun!
   Enjoy yourselves!

2. Have you two met each other?

► A group of people are at the airport, waiting for a tour to depart. Listen to the conversation and complete the chart.

	Ted	Marie	Julia	John
Who used to work together?	√	√		
Who teaches at Kennedy High School?				
Who is from the same hometown?				
Who went to college together?				

► **Say how the people know each other.**
Ted and Marie used to work together.

► **Listen to the conversation.**
► **In groups of four, practice the conversation.**

John Hi, Julia. Have you met Ted?
Julia Yes, I have. We both teach at Kennedy High School. How are you doing, Ted?
Ted Hi, Julia. Nice to see you.
John Julia, have you met Marie?
Julia No, I haven't.
John This is Marie Jones. Marie has her own advertising agency. Marie, I'd like you to meet Julia Rivera. Julia's a teacher. She and I are from the same hometown.
Marie Nice to meet you, Julia.

► **Interview three classmates and take notes.
Ask the questions below or your own questions.**

1. Where are you from originally?
2. Where do you work?/Where do you live?
3. How long have you been at this school?

► **Now listen to the two possible conversations.**
► **Introduce the classmates you interviewed above.**

A Have you two met each other?

B No, I don't believe we have.

A Alex, this is Amy Tang. Amy's from Taiwan. Amy, I'd like you to meet Alex Garcia. Alex is from California.
B Nice to meet you, Amy.

C Nice to meet you, too.

B Yes, we have. We were in the same class last term.

4 Unit 1

▶ **Listen to the two possible conversations.**
▶ **Work with a partner. Find out if your partner has been to these or other cities.**

San Francisco

Rio de Janeiro

Bangkok

A Have you ever been to San Francisco?

B Yes, I've been there many times. Have you?   **B** No, I never have. Have you?

A Yes, I was just there last week.   **A** No, I haven't.

I've been there	once. twice. a few times. many times.

▶ **Study the frames:** The present perfect

Yes-no questions

Have	I you we they	**met** Julia? **been** to San Francisco?
Has	he she	

Short answers

Yes,	you I	**have**.
No,	we they	**haven't**.
Yes,	he	**has**.
No,	she	**hasn't**.

Past participles of some irregular verbs

Base form	Simple past	Past participle
be (am, is, are)	was, were	**been**
do	did	**done**
eat	ate	**eaten**
go	went	**gone**
have	had	**had**
hear	heard	**heard**
leave	left	**left**
meet	met	**met**
read [rid]	read [rɛd]	**read** [rɛd]
ride	rode	**ridden**
see	saw	**seen**
take	took	**taken**

▶ **Complete the conversation. Use the present perfect of the verbs in parentheses or short answers.**
▶ **Listen to check your work.**

Marie *Have you taken* (take) a tour before?
Julia Yes, *I have* . I went to Europe with a group last year. _____ (be) to Europe?
Marie Yes, _____ , but only to London on business. I'm really excited about this trip.
Julia Me too. _____ (see) all the brochures?
Marie Yes. I can't wait to see all those places. By the way, _____ (meet) Scott, our tour guide?
Julia No, _____. I think he's Australian. What do you know about him?
Marie Not much. _____ (hear) this is his second or third tour, and everybody seems to like him. Come on and I'll introduce you.
Julia Great.

▶ **In small groups, make a list of the different countries your classmates have been to. Then, under the name of each country, write the names of the cities your classmates have visited.**

3. Have you ever gone snorkeling?

TALK ABOUT THINGS YOU'VE DONE • PRESENT PERFECT

▶ Find out which tour the group is going on. Listen to the radio commercial and circle *Pacific Tour A* or *Pacific Tour B*.

Pacific Tours

Tour A

San Francisco, California, U.S.A.   *1 day*
- see the Golden Gate Bridge
- ride on old-fashioned cable cars
- walk through Chinatown

Malaysia   *3 days*
- walk along tropical beaches
- try water sports like scuba diving
- taste fabulous seafood and exotic fruits

Australia   *9 days*
- go swimming and surfing in the best surf in the Pacific
- go snorkeling or scuba diving at the Great Barrier Reef
- climb Ayers Rock and watch the sun rise

Japan   *5 days*
- visit Tokyo's famous temples and shrines
- go shopping in the Ginza district
- take a ride on a Bullet Train to Mt. Fuji and spend the day hiking up this famous mountain

Tour B

San Francisco, California, U.S.A.   *1 day*
- see the Golden Gate Bridge
- ride on old-fashioned cable cars
- walk through Chinatown

Malaysia   *3 days*
- walk along tropical beaches
- try water sports like scuba diving
- taste fabulous seafood and exotic fruits

Australia   *9 days*
- see the famous Sydney Opera House
- take photos from the Harbour Bridge
- spend days on the beach and evenings at Sydney's restaurants and pubs

Thailand   *3 days*
- tour the exotic temples and palaces of old Siam
- see the unique floating market
- shop for silk and handicrafts in Bangkok's fascinating markets

▶ Work with a partner. Find out if your partner has done any of the things described in the two tours.

A *Have you ever gone snorkeling?*
B *No, I haven't. Have you?*
A *. . .*

▶ Plan a trip. Work in small groups. Imagine you are going to take one of the tours above. Decide which tour to take. Tell the class which tour you chose and why.

4. Let me help you with that.

► **Complete each exchange with an offer from the box.**
► **Listen to check your work.**

Let me help you . . .

a. get those down.
b. put that up.
c. carry something.
d. move that.

► **Listen to the conversations. Does the person accept or decline the offer?**

Accept   Decline
1.   √
2.
3.
4.

► **Listen to the two possible conversations.**
► **Practice the conversations with a partner.**

Other ways to say it

Would you like some help with . . . ?
Can I help you with that?

A Here, let me help you with that.

B Oh, thanks. That's very kind of you.   **B** That's all right. I can manage.

Some ways to accept help	Some ways to decline help
Thanks. That's very kind of you.	I'm all set. But thanks anyway.
I appreciate it.	That's all right. I can manage.
That's really nice of you.	That's O.K. I've got it.

► **Work with a partner. Act out the conversation.**
Student A: Imagine you are the person in the picture.
Student B: Offer to help.

5. I see you're reading *Time* magazine.

 ▶ These people are traveling on trains, planes, and buses. Listen to the four conversations. Write the number of the conversation next to the correct picture.

 ▶ Listen to the conversation and practice it with a partner.
▶ Strike up a conversation and try to keep it going.

A I hear you've got a new job.
B Yes, I just started.

Some ways to strike up a conversation	Some ways to respond
With anyone:	
I see you're wearing a T-shirt from Temple University.	Yes, I go to school there.
I see you're reading *Time* magazine.	Yes, I just picked it up.
That's an interesting necklace.	Thanks. It's from Mexico.
With someone you know:	
I hear you got a new job.	Yes, I just started.
I hear you went to Brazil.	Yes, I just got back.

▶ **Two people are on a flight from Toronto to New York. Play the roles below.**

Student A: You live in New York. You arrange concert tours for musicians. You've been on a business trip.

1. Start a conversation with the person next to you. The person is reading *The Wall Street Journal*.
2. Find out where the person is from.
3. Find out what kind of work the person does.
4. Find out if the person has been to New York before.
5. Continue the conversation, answer the other person's question, and tell about yourself.

Student B: You're on a business trip to the U.S. The person next to you starts a conversation.

1. You live in Montreal.
2. You work for a Canadian company that makes stereo equipment.
3. You spent a year in Toronto studying sound engineering.
4. Find out if the person next to you has ever been to Montreal.
5. Continue the conversation, answer the other person's questions, and tell about yourself.

 ▶ **Work with a partner. Listen to these two conversations. Decide which conversation ends and which one continues.**

1. **A** It's been nice talking to you.
   B I've enjoyed talking to you, too.
   A Enjoy your stay in New York.
   B Thanks, I will.

2. **B** Have you ever been to Montreal?
   A No, but I'd like to go there. My friends say the night life is great there.
   B It is! We have terrific nightclubs and restaurants.
   A Really?

▶ **Imagine that you are traveling on an airplane. Strike up a conversation with a partner. Find out where your partner is from and where he or she is going. Tell a little about yourself. Then end the conversation.**

Some ways to end a conversation	Other ways to say it
I've enjoyed talking to you. It's been nice talking to you. Enjoy your trip (your stay)! Enjoy yourself (yourselves)!	Have fun! Have a good time!

6. How have you been?

Laura Enders runs into a friend outside her health club.

1

Roger Laura!

Laura Oh, hi, Roger.

Roger How have you been?

Laura Fine.

Roger I hear you went back to Seattle for a few days.

Laura Yes, I just got back yesterday.

Roger Did you have a nice visit?

Laura Really nice. It was good being back home and just relaxing. My brother Mark was there, too. You've met Mark, haven't you?

Roger Sure. I met him when he was here in Chicago last year. What's he up to these days? Still playing the guitar?

Laura Yes. As a matter of fact, he just started his own band. How's everything with you and Carol?

Roger Great.

Laura How are the kids?

Roger They're both fine.

Laura Gee, I haven't seen them in so long. They must be really big.

Roger Well, why don't you come over sometime? Carol and the kids would love to see you.

Laura I'll do that. I'll give Carol a call during the week.

2. Figure it out

Say *True, False,* or *It doesn't say.*

1. Laura knows Roger and his family.
2. Laura just visited Seattle.
3. Roger knows Mark.
4. Laura plays the guitar.
5. Laura just called Roger's wife.

3. Listen in

Read the statement below. Then listen to another conversation taking place nearby. Choose *a, b,* or *c.*

These people are talking mainly about _____.

a. a play
b. a movie
c. an actor

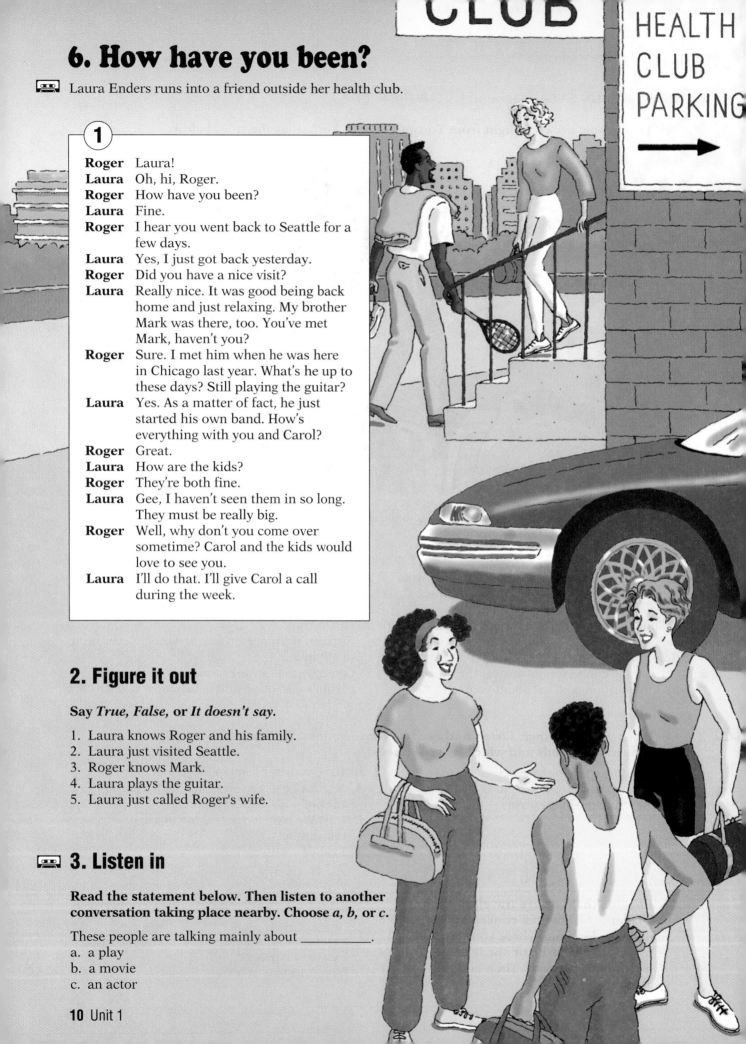

7. Your turn

Work in groups. Discuss places you've visited and things you've done. Read the sample conversation before you begin.

A Have you ever been to Mexico City?
B Yes. I went with some friends last summer.
A How did you like it?
B It was beautiful. Have you ever been there?
A No, but I'd like to go someday.

Mexico City is the largest city in the world.

Elephants are found in the wild in parts of Africa and Asia. Most people see them in zoos, such as this one in San Diego, California.

Thousands of fans attend rock concerts. Although many new groups are popular, some older bands and musicians, such as Eric Clapton, still attract large crowds.

Euro Disney is one of the four internationally popular Disney amusement parks around the world. There is also a Disney park in Japan, as well as two in the U.S.—one in California and one in Florida.

Windsurfing is a sport that combines the skills of surfing and sailing. Here, windsurfers enjoy the waters off the coast of Brazil.

How to say it

Practice the past participles and phrases. Then practice the exchanges. Ask questions using the phrases.

been [bɪn]	. . . been to Euro Disney?
seen [sin]	. . . seen an elephant?
gone [gɔn]	. . . gone to a soccer game?

had [hæd]	. . . had a desire to travel?
eaten [ítn]	. . . eaten at a McDonald's?
read [rɛd]	. . . read anything by Stephen King?

A Have you ever been to Euro Disney?
B Yes, I have.

A Have you ever seen an elephant?
B No, I haven't.

8.

GETAWAY EMPLOYEE OF THE MONTH

Getaway *magazine spoke with Josef Schmidt, our travel agent in Hamburg, Germany, about his many travels.*

GETAWAY: We hear you've traveled to nearly forty different countries. Tell us, what has been your favorite place to visit?

SCHMIDT: Oh, I'd have to say Prague. I've always loved exploring old cities, and Prague is one of the most beautiful in terms of architecture. There are fantastic castles and museums that are relatively unknown to most tourists.

GETAWAY: Is there any one place that is particularly memorable for you?

SCHMIDT: That would probably be northern Mali, in the Sahara Desert. I spent New Year's Eve there once, and I remember watching the sun set over the sand dunes. When the stars came out, they were incredibly bright. I felt very far from home but very close to nature. It was completely different from any place I've ever been.

GETAWAY: What's your next destination?

SCHMIDT: I'm thinking about Australia. I've never been there. I'd love to go to the Great Barrier Reef and do some diving. And I've always wanted to see the Sydney Opera House.

GETAWAY: Of course they speak English in Australia, but how do you deal with all the different languages in other places you visit?

SCHMIDT: Well, I learned German at home and English at school. I find that I can pick up many phrases and expressions as I travel. If I know I'll be staying in one country for a while, I try to get a book or tape of the language to study. I'm fluent in Italian now, but I've also picked up quite a bit of Spanish, French, and Russian along the way.

GETAWAY: Has there been any place where you've had a lot of trouble with the language?

SCHMIDT: I was in China last year and yes, I had some difficulty there. Chinese is so very different from the languages I've studied, and of course the writing system is completely different. I had to use a lot of gestures and sign language.

GETAWAY: Is it hard to adjust to the different customs and people you meet?

SCHMIDT: I go with an open mind. I like to try new things. The first thing I always do when I get to a new place is buy a map. Then I'm ready to start on my new adventure.

The Old City of Prague

1. Scan the article for answers to these questions.

1. How many countries has Josef Schmidt been to?
2. How many languages does he speak?

2. Discuss these questions in a group.

1. On which continent do you think Josef Schmidt has done most of his traveling?
2. How does he prepare for his travels? Do you think his preparations are useful?
3. How do you adjust to different languages and customs when you travel or meet foreign tourists?

FUNCTIONS/THEMES	LANGUAGE	FORMS
Talk about jobs and places you've lived	How long have you lived in Clinton? For three years. How long have you worked as a hairstylist? Since high school.	The present perfect information questions and statements with *for* and *since* The present perfect vs. the simple past tense
Talk about your fantasies	I've always wanted to go hiking in the Himalayas.	The present perfect
Talk about your family	Do you have any brothers and sisters? I have four older brothers and two older sisters. I'm the youngest. Two of them live in California. The others live in Chicago.	Partitives, *the other one,* and *the others*

Preview the conversations.

Clinton Students Start Summer Jobs

CLINTON, July 1—Summer has started, but Clinton college students and recent high school graduates are spending their vacations working. Ann Rutgers, the manager of Templine, a temporary employment agency, notes that many of the students are working to help pay for their college tuition and the others want to work for the experience.

"I've done office work for the last two summers," said Donna Lucas. "It's a little boring, but it's a change from schoolwork."

Jim Wright couldn't find a job in the construction business, so he took this job as a waiter in a local restaurant. "I've never worked as a waiter before," Jim said, "so I'm not sure if I'm going to like it or not. Ask me again at the end of the summer."

May Huang is working as a volunteer at a summer camp. "I've always wanted to work with kids," May told the reporter. "I'm getting great experience."

Read the article and discuss the questions.
1. Do high school and college students in your country have jobs during vacations?
2. If so, what kind of jobs do they have?
3. Have you ever had a temporary job?
4. If so, tell a partner what you did and if you enjoyed it.

9. How long have you been a waitress?

Tina Marco is starting a summer job as a waitress at Frank's Restaurant.

A

Marge Hi. You must be the new waitress. I'm Marge.
Tina Hi, Marge. I'm Tina.
Marge Do you go to Clinton High, Tina?
Tina I'm starting this fall. I'll be a senior. I've only lived here since the beginning of June.
Marge Really? Where did you live before?
Tina Texas.
Marge Well, welcome to Clinton.
Tina Thanks.

B

Tina How long have you lived in Clinton?
Marge Me? My whole life. You know Frank, the owner? We've known each other for thirty-five years . . . since kindergarten.
Tina No kidding! Have you ever wanted to live somewhere else?
Marge When I was younger I wanted to move to Hollywood and be an actress. But here I am . . . still in Clinton and still a waitress.
Tina Oh, that's funny. I've always wanted to be an actress, too. How long have you been a waitress?
Marge For twenty years now.
Tina That's a long time.
Marge You're telling me. I've always wanted to try a different kind of work. I make pretty good money as a waitress, though, so I just never have.
Tina Where else have you worked, or have you always worked here?
Marge Oh, no. Frank's only had this place since last year. Before that, I worked at the Clinton Hotel.

C

Joe Hi, Tina. How's it going?

Tina Oh, Joe, hi!

Marge Who's that good-looking guy? Your boyfriend?

Tina No. That's my brother Joe.

Marge Is he older or younger than you?

Tina He's a year older. I'm the youngest in the family.

Marge Oh, so you have other brothers and sisters . . .

Tina Yes, I have two other older brothers besides Joe and one older sister. But none of them live at home anymore.

Marge Oh, are they all married?

Tina Only my oldest brother, Tony. The others are away at college.

Marge I've always wanted to have brothers and sisters.

Tina You don't have any?

Marge No, I'm an only child.

Figure it out

1. Listen to the conversations. Then choose the correct sentence.

1. Tina is a student and has a temporary job as a waitress.
2. Tina has been a waitress for a long time.

2. Listen again. Are the statements about *Marge*, *Tina*, or *Both* of them?

1. She has three older brothers.   *Tina.*
2. She has lived in Clinton all her life.
3. She works for Frank.
4. She is in high school.
5. She is an only child.
6. She lived in Texas before.

3. Match.

1. Marge and Frank have known each other ————— a. since last year.
2. Marge has lived in Clinton
3. Tina has lived in Clinton
4. Frank has owned his restaurant

a. since last year.
b. for thirty-five years.
c. her whole life.
d. since the beginning of June.

10. How long have you lived in Clinton?

▶ Listen and select the employment application of the person being interviewed.

Name John Hill
Position Desired Store Manager

Current Position Manager
Puppy Love Pet Shop, Clinton

1 year — since he moved here

Previous Experience Salesclerk
Best Pets, Toronto

Education Seneca College
Toronto

Name Paul Jacobs
Position Desired Hair Stylist

Current Position Hair Stylist
New Wave Beauty Salon
Clinton

3 years

Previous Experience Hair Stylist
Kindest Cuts
Washington, D.C.

Education Martin Luther King
High School
Washington, D.C.

▶ Listen to the conversation and practice it with a partner.
▶ Act out a similar conversation with information from the other application in exercise 1.

A How long have you lived in Clinton?
B For three years.
A Where did you live before?
B In Washington, D.C.
A Where are you working now?
B At New Wave Beauty Salon.
A How long have you worked there?
B Since I moved to Clinton. Before that, I worked at Kindest Cuts in Washington.

▶ Study the frames: The present perfect

Information questions					Statements with *for* and *since*				
	have	you they	**worked**	at New Wave?	I We	**'ve**	**worked**	at New Wave	
How long			**lived**	in Clinton?	They He		**lived**	in Clinton	for two years. since high school.
	has	he she	**wanted**	to move?	She	**'s**	**wanted**	to move	

The past participle of regular verbs is the same as the simple past tense form.

have 've
has 's
he's = he is *or* he has
she's = she is *or* she has

▶ Complete the conversation with information questions and *for* or *since*.
▶ Listen to check your work.

Ray You did a great job on that last customer, Paul. _____ (be) a hairstylist?

Paul _____ I finished high school. I worked at New Wave before, but I've wanted to work here for a long time.

Ray Well, I hope you stay here.

Paul _____ (had) this business?

Ray _____ we moved here from Washington, D.C., about six years ago. Lois and I lived in Washington _____ a few years before we came to Clinton.

Paul Oh, yeah? I lived in Washington before, too. I worked at Kindest Cuts.

Ray I know that place. Did you work with Jean Martin?

Paul Sure I did. _____ (know) Jean?

Ray _____ we were kids. We still keep in touch.

▶ Study the frame: The present perfect vs. the simple past tense

The present perfect: something that began in the past and continues into the present	The simple past tense: something completed in the past
Paul has been a hairstylist since he finished high school. (He is a hairstylist now.)	He worked at New Wave before. (He doesn't work there anymore.)
Ray has lived in Clinton for six years. (He still lives in Clinton.)	He lived in Washington, D.C., for a few years. (He doesn't live in Washington anymore.)

▶ Listen to Ray talk about himself. Then put the events in order.

_____ moved to Clinton
_____ got jobs in Hollywood
_____ got married to Lois
_____ moved to California

_____ moved back to Washington, D.C.
_____ got the salon in Clinton
_1_ graduated from high school
_____ got into the hairstyling business

▶ Tell a classmate about Ray.

Ray's been in the hairstyling business for thirty years.
He got his first job right after high school.

▶ Interview two classmates. Find out where they've lived and what they've done.

Other ways to say it	
for . . .	since . . .
ten years	1992
a long time	I left school

11. I've always wanted to be a rock star.

1 ▶ **Work with a partner. Look at the pictures and guess who has always wanted to**

_____ be a rock star.
_____ go hiking in the Himalayas.
_____ work in the construction business.
_____ write TV soap operas.

▶ **Listen and match the people with their fantasies.**

1 Ellen Hanson
Bookkeeper
London, England

2 Luigi Contini
Systems Analyst
Rome, Italy

3 Carol Valentine
Graphic Artist
Atlanta, Georgia

4 Peter Yang
College Teacher
Taipei, Taiwan

2 ▶ **Listen to the conversations and practice them with a partner.**

1. A I've always wanted to go hiking in the Himalayas.
   B Really? You know, I've always wanted to travel, too.

2. A I've always wanted to write TV soap operas.
   B That's funny. I've always wanted to be in show business, too.

3 ▶ **Work with a partner. Look at the pictures below and act out conversations like the ones in exercise 2.**

4 ▶ **Talk to two classmates. Find out where they have always wanted to go or what they have always wanted to do. Report to the class.**

Luisa has always wanted to take flying lessons.
Ali has always wanted to go to Italy.

12. Do you have any brothers and sisters?

1 ► **Listen and label the picture with the names.**

a. Rose
b. Carl
c. Sue
d. Frank
e. Pat (the speaker)

2 ► **Listen to the two possible conversations and practice them with a partner.**
► **Act out a similar conversation with your partner. Use your own information.**

A Do you have any brothers and sisters?

B I have four older brothers and two older sisters. I'm the youngest in the family.

B No, I'm an only child.

I'm . . .
the middle child
the oldest
the youngest
. . . in the family.

3 ► **Study the frame: Partitives, *the other one*, and *the others***

Pat Martin has four brothers.	**All** of them are married. **None** of them live in Clinton. **Two** of them live in California. **The others** live in Chicago.
She has two sisters.	**Both** of them are in college. **One** of them lives at school. **The other one** lives at home.
She has a lot of nieces and nephews.	**Most** of them live in California. **Some** of them were born there.

Partitives show what part of a whole something is.

100%	all, both
	most
	many
	some
0%	none

4 ► **Complete the newspaper article. Choose the correct words.**
► **Listen to check your work.**

5 ► **Interview two classmates about their families. Report to the class.**

Pedro has a younger brother and a younger sister. Both of them live at home.

The Martin family held their second reunion in Clinton last weekend. _____ (Many/One) of the children have moved away from Clinton, but _____ (both/all) of them showed up for the party. _____ (One/Most) of the Martins' children are married and _____ (none/all) of their grandchildren are over ten years old, so it was a noisy and happy event. Bill and Jane Martin have lived in Clinton for forty years now. They held their first family reunion eight years ago, after their youngest son moved to Chicago. "_____ (Both/Most) of our reunions have been fun," said Bill, "but this one is special because of all our new grandchildren." "_____ (The others/ The other one) seemed awfully quiet," laughed Jane. We managed to talk with one grandchild, David Martin, age 4. "Great party," he assured us. _____ (The others/The other one) were all too busy to comment.

13. I see from your résumé. . .

Bill Dow is interviewing Doug Lee for a job as the director of a recreation program for teenagers. Mr. Dow runs the Community Services Agency.

1

Mr. Dow Mr. Lee, I see from your résumé that you've had a lot of experience in sales.

Doug Yes, my parents have a store. They sell housewares. I used to work there after school.

Mr. Dow Well, what kind of work have you done with adolescents?

Doug I taught swimming for a couple of summers at camp. A lot of the campers were in their early teens. Then I taught high school physical education, and I've been a guidance counselor in the Seattle public school system for the last three years.

Mr. Dow Why are you thinking of leaving your present job?

Doug Well, I enjoy counseling, but I miss athletics. This job would give me a chance to do both of them. And I feel, too, that I'm ready for a change. I've lived in Seattle my whole life.

Mr. Dow So you think you'd like living in Chicago?

Doug Very much. I've always wanted to live here.

Mr. Dow Well, Mr. Lee, you seem to have some good qualifications for the job. We're interviewing all this week, so I'll let you know in ten days or so. While you're here, I'd also like you to meet . . . (*Knock at the door*)

2. Figure it out

Say *True, False,* or *It doesn't say.*

1. Doug used to teach swimming.
2. Doug has worked with teenagers before.
3. Doug is a physical education teacher now.
4. Doug taught physical education for three years.
5. Doug likes sports.
6. Mr. Dow will call or write Doug in about ten days.
7. Mr. Dow is going to interview two other people for the job.

3. Listen in

Kate Simmons is a social worker at the Community Services Agency. Read the questions below. Then listen to the conversation and answer the questions.

1. How long has Kate worked at the Community Services Agency?
2. How long have Kate and Doug known each other?
3. Where did they meet?

14. Your turn

Here's a page from the Clinton High School Yearbook of twenty years ago. One of these people became a firefighter, one a teacher, and one an international spy.

Read about the people, and then work in groups to guess their professions. Discuss the reasons for their choices. Read the conversation before you begin.

A I think Phyllis became a teacher.
B Why?
A Because she's always liked being with people.
B I see what you mean. And she's wanted to travel since she was in high school. Teachers have long vacations.

Phyllis Sandler

Awards and Activities:
President—Great Books Club
Sarah Davis Science Award
Best Quality: Good conversationalist
Likes: People, people, people
Dislikes: Staying up late at night
Ambition: To visit a new country
every year
People say:
"She's got a great sense of humor, even about herself."
"She's extremely patient—she explained chemistry to me."

David Simon

Awards and Activities:
Marathon champion
Secretary—Great Books Club
Best Quality: Fantastic memory
Likes: Learning about new things
Dislikes: Making conversation with
people he doesn't know
Ambition: To save money to buy a
small country house
People say:
"He's incredibly well organized. I always borrowed his notes." "He seems shy, but he's fun."

Melina Spanos

Awards and Activities:
Best Actress
President—French Club
Best Quality: Common sense
Likes: New people, new places
Dislikes: Being alone
Ambition: To retire early and write
a book
People say:
"She's a great listener. People always tell her their problems . . . and she never repeats anything." "She feels comfortable in the most difficult situations."

How to say it

Practice the words. Then practice the conversation.

talked	studied	started
[t]	[d]	[əd]

A Have you talked to Mary?
B Yes, I talked to her last night.
A Has she started her music class?
B Yes, she started it last week.
A Has she studied music before?
B Well, she studied piano when she was younger.

15. A Changing Work Force

Before you read this article, look at exercise 1. Try to guess the answers. Then read the article to see if you were right.

Is the work force changing in American life? According to statistics, America's skilled white-collar work force has overtaken the ranks of skilled blue-collar workers for the first time. Those who worry that America is becoming a nation of lawyers may have some evidence: There are now 1.4 lawyers for every farmer, whereas twenty-five years ago there were 4.5 farmers for every lawyer. Other occupations on the rise are computer analysts, doctors, police officers, and psychologists.

While women have shown steady advancement and upward mobility, their share of jobs in traditionally male roles is still relatively low. For example, the proportion of women doctors is less than one-third, while the percentage of women nurses (a typically female vocation) is still about 90%. Women represent only 3% of firefighters, 27% of veterinarians, and 15% of police officers.

Certain occupations have declined overall in recent years. The number of jobs held by barbers, elevator operators, and farmers has been steadily shrinking. Other occupations with decreasing numbers: rail workers, tailors, and English professors.

1. Complete the tables below. Use these occupations:

nurses
police officers
tailors
doctors
elevator operators
rail workers
firefighters

English professors
computer analysts
barbers
psychologists
veterinarians
farmers
lawyers

WOMEN AT WORK

Women at work represent less than 50% of:

_____
_____
_____
_____

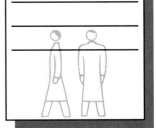

JOBS ON THE RISE

Occupations that are growing:

_____
_____
_____
_____

Women at work represent more than 50% of:

_____
_____

JOBS IN DECLINE

Occupations that are decreasing:

_____
_____
_____
_____

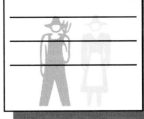

2. In your country, are there any jobs held mostly by men? Mostly by women? Is the situation changing? In what ways?

PREVIEW

FUNCTIONS/THEMES	LANGUAGE	FORMS
Give an opinion	I've heard it's not that great. It's supposed to be excellent. Was it any good? I thought so. I didn't think so.	
Talk about plans Talk about things you've done and haven't done	Some (A few, A couple) of us are getting together Saturday night. We're thinking of going to the Picasso exhibit. I haven't seen it. I've already seen it. I've never heard of it. I haven't seen it yet. Why don't you join us? I'd like to, but I might have to work. I'd like to, but I might not be in town.	The present perfect: negative statements The present perfect with *already, never,* and *not . . . yet* The present perfect vs. the simple past tense *Might* and *might not*
Make suggestions	Why don't you see the new play at the Orpheum?	

Preview the conversations.

Are you going to be around this weekend?

Yes, I think so.

Oh, I've already seen it.

Wynton Marsalis in concert at The Green Door. Tues. through Sun. shows at 9 & 11 p.m. For ticket information, call 555-2243

Read the ad. Then continue the conversation between Bob and Carol.

Bob

You have two tickets to the Wynton Marsalis concert for Saturday night. Invite Carol to go with you. If she's already seen the concert, ask her opinion of it.

Carol

You went to the Wynton Marsalis concert last night and really enjoyed it. Bob has two tickets. Decide if you want to go again. If not, suggest a student in the class that Bob can invite.

16. Some of us are getting together.

 Some friends are making plans for the weekend.

A

Claire Anything exciting going on this weekend?

Janet Oh, look, Wynton Marsalis is in town.

Charlie Who's Wynton Marsalis? I've never heard of him.

Janet What? He's one of the greatest jazz musicians in the world!

Claire The tickets must cost a fortune. Are there any good movies?

Janet Well, there's a classic film festival. They're showing *La Dolce Vita*. It's supposed to be excellent.

Claire I've never seen it, but I'd like to. Why don't we go Saturday night?

Charlie I've already seen it.

Claire You have?

Charlie I just saw it the night before last.

Claire Was it any good?

Charlie I thought so. I think it's Fellini's best film.

B

Janet Let's see what's playing at the State. Oh, look . . . it's a James Bond movie. It's supposed to be really good.

Claire Fine with me. Charlie?

Charlie We could go dancing.

Janet Listen, I think we'll have to talk later. I've got to go now.

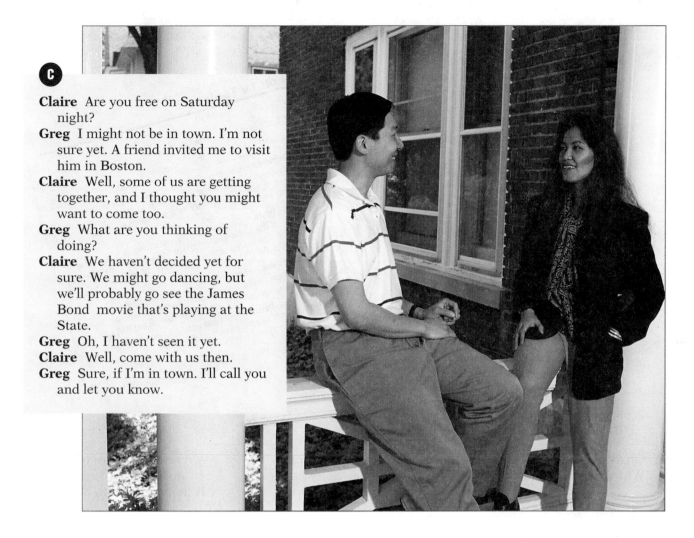

C

Claire Are you free on Saturday night?

Greg I might not be in town. I'm not sure yet. A friend invited me to visit him in Boston.

Claire Well, some of us are getting together, and I thought you might want to come too.

Greg What are you thinking of doing?

Claire We haven't decided yet for sure. We might go dancing, but we'll probably go see the James Bond movie that's playing at the State.

Greg Oh, I haven't seen it yet.

Claire Well, come with us then.

Greg Sure, if I'm in town. I'll call you and let you know.

Figure it out

1. Listen to the conversations. Then choose a, b, or c.

1. a. Janet has heard of Wynton Marsalis.
   b. Janet hasn't heard of Wynton Marsalis.
   c. Both Janet and Charlie have heard of Wynton Marsalis.

2. a. Janet wants to see the James Bond movie.
   b. Charlie wants to see the James Bond movie.
   c. Both Janet and Charlie want to see the James Bond movie.

3. a. Greg is going to be in town on Saturday night.
   b. Greg might be in town on Saturday night.
   c. Greg isn't going to be in town on Saturday night.

2. Listen again and say *True, False,* or *It doesn't say.*

1. Wynton Marsalis is a famous jazz musician.
2. The tickets to the Wynton Marsalis concert are probably expensive.
3. Charlie liked *La Dolce Vita*.
4. Janet has seen *La Dolce Vita*.
5. Claire and her friends are going dancing Saturday night.
6. Greg doesn't want to see the James Bond movie.
7. Greg is going to call Claire later.

3. Find another way to say it.

1. I don't know who he is.   *I've never heard of him.*
2. two nights ago
3. What did you think of it?
4. I'll tell you.
5. a lot of money
6. I've heard it's really good.
7. Maybe we'll go dancing.

17. I've heard it's not that great.

1 ► Two people are talking about a movie. Listen to the conversation and circle the title of the movie.

Movies on TV Tonight

Movie Ratings

★ ★ ★ ★ Excellent

★ ★ ★ Good ★ ★ Fair

★ Poor

Somewhere in the Past – A young man receives a mysterious watch that allows him to travel to the past. A fascinating story with a beautiful ending. **8:00 PM (5)**

City Lights – Charlie Chaplin's masterpiece tells the story of the Little Tramp's love for a blind flower girl and his friendship with a millionaire. A wonderful movie. **9:00 PM (2)**

Casablanca – Humphrey Bogart and Ingrid Bergman star in one of the most popular films of all time. Romance, excitement, and suspense. **9:00 PM (7)**

One Horse Town – The best acting comes from the horse in this tired Western. Don't bother. **11:30 PM (7)**

2 ► Listen to the three possible conversations.
► Act out similar conversations with a partner.

A Are there any good movies on TV?
B Well, *Somewhere in the Past* is on channel 5.

A Oh, it's supposed to be good. Why don't we watch that?	**A** Oh, not that. I've heard it's not that great. See what's on the other channels.	**A** I've never heard of it. Is it any good? **B** It's supposed to be.

Some opinions

I've heard it's not that great.
I've heard it's exciting.
It's supposed to be excellent.
It's supposed to be boring.

3 ► Listen to the two possible conversations.
► Work with a partner. Act out similar conversations about novels, movies, and music albums you know.

A I just read Stephen King's latest novel.
B Was it any good?

A I thought so. **A** I didn't think so.

Other ways to say it	
What did you think of it? How did you like it?	I enjoyed it a lot. I thought it was very good.
How was it?	I didn't like it at all.

a novel

a movie

a music album

18. I'm thinking of going to the Picasso exhibit.

1 ▶ Listen to the conversation. Which two things do the people talk about? Circle the ads.

Picasso Exhibit
50 paintings and sculptures
May 1–28
The Modern Art Institute

All the Way Home
A new play by Erica Howard
Orpheum Theater
Monday–Saturday
8:00 p.m.

K I S M E T
Fine Indian Cuisine
65 Park Street
555-4749
Dinner: Monday–Saturday

CITY CENTER
Now Through May 9
Odyssey
Dance Company
Box office 555-5348

The Continental Club
presents
Sounds of Jamaica
live reggae music
May 8–10 • 8 PM

New World Circus
PARKSIDE STADIUM
May 6–18
10:30 AM, 2:30 PM, 7:30 PM

2 ▶ Listen to the two possible conversations.
▶ Work with a partner. Act out similar conversations about the ads.

A We're thinking of going to the Picasso exhibit on Saturday.

B Oh, I've already seen it.
A You have?
B Yeah, I just saw it last weekend.

B Oh, I haven't seen it yet.
A Why don't you come with us then?
B Sure. I'd love to.

3 ▶ Study the frames: The present perfect

Negative statements			
I You We They	**haven't**	**seen**	it.
He She	**hasn't**		

Present perfect with *already,*
never, and *not . . . yet*

I've **already** seen it.

She's **never** heard of it.

I haven't seen it **yet**.

4 ▶ Listen to the conversation.
▶ Act out similar conversations with your own information.

A Some of us are getting together Saturday night. Do you want to join us?
B Well, I'd like to, but I might have to work. I'll call you and let you know.

I might . . .

have to work.
have other plans.
be out of town.
not have time.
not be free.
not be in town.

Some of us
A couple of us
A few of us

19. Have you been to a sumo match yet?

a sumo match

people eating at a sushi bar

a Kabuki performance

a bullet train

the Tokyo Tower

a Japanese tea ceremony

▶ **A travel agent and a customer are talking about things to do in Tokyo. Listen to the conversation and number the pictures in the order you hear them.**

▶ **Listen to the two possible conversations.**
▶ **Imagine you are visiting Tokyo for a week. A Japanese friend is asking what you've done. Act out similar conversations using the information below.**

A Have you been to a sumo match yet?

B Yes. As a matter of fact, I went to one last night.

B No. I haven't been to one yet, but I might go to one tomorrow.

> You can use *one* as a pronoun.
> go to **a** sumo match > go to **one**

THINGS TO DO IN TOKYO	Done?	When?
go to a sumo match	✓	last night
see a Kabuki play		maybe tomorrow night
take the bullet train		maybe tomorrow
see a tea ceremony	✓	two days ago
go to Tokyo Tower	✓	yesterday afternoon
try sushi or sashimi		maybe for dinner

▶ **Study the frame: The present perfect vs. the simple past tense**

Use the present perfect to refer to an *unspecified* time in the past:

Have you **seen** a Kabuki play?
Yes, I**'ve** already **seen** one.

Use the simple past tense to refer to a *specific* time in the past:

When **did** you **see** it?
I **saw** it last night.

Use present perfect negative statements with *yet* to refer to something that didn't happen in the past but still might happen. Compare:

I haven't seen a Kabuki play yet. (But I might see one.)
I didn't see a Kabuki play when I was in Japan. (I'm not in Japan anymore.)

Use *yet* when you expect something to happen:

Have you seen a Kabuki play yet?
I haven't seen a Kabuki play yet. (But I plan to see one.)

► **Nancy and Victor are visitors in Mexico City. Complete the conversation with the present perfect or the simple past tense of the verbs in parentheses.**
► **Listen to check your work.**

Pyramid of the Sun Teotihuacán

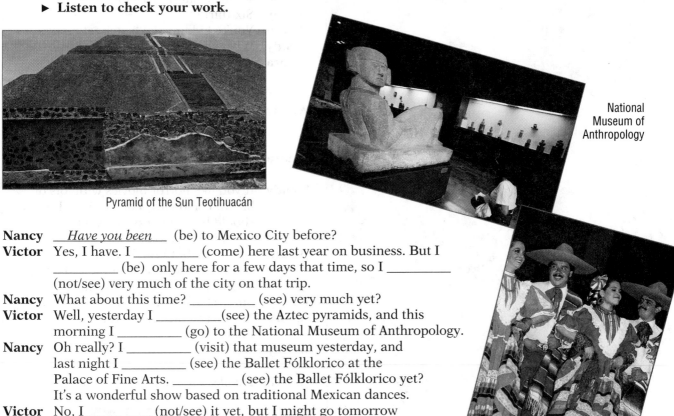

National Museum of Anthropology

Ballet Fólklorico

Nancy _Have you been_ (be) to Mexico City before?

Victor Yes, I have. I _____ (come) here last year on business. But I _____ (be) only here for a few days that time, so I _____ (not/see) very much of the city on that trip.

Nancy What about this time? _____ (see) very much yet?

Victor Well, yesterday I _____ (see) the Aztec pyramids, and this morning I _____ (go) to the National Museum of Anthropology.

Nancy Oh really? I _____ (visit) that museum yesterday, and last night I _____ (see) the Ballet Fólklorico at the Palace of Fine Arts. _____ (see) the Ballet Fólklorico yet? It's a wonderful show based on traditional Mexican dances.

Victor No, I _____ (not/see) it yet, but I might go tomorrow night. I've heard it's very hard to get tickets.

Nancy Sometimes it is, but maybe you'll be lucky.

MAKE SUGGESTIONS

► **Listen to the two possible conversations and practice them with a partner.**

A Why don't you see the new play at the Orpheum?

B I've already seen it.   **B** Good idea. I haven't seen it yet.

A You have? When did you go?

B I just went on Tuesday.

► **Make a list of things to do in your town. Complete the chart.**
► **Work with a partner. Student A: You are a tourist. Student B: Make suggestions about things to do on the chart.**

Places to go and things to do:
Museums:
Sports:
Movies:
Music:
Other activities:

20. Can I let you know?

Laura is having a cup of coffee with her friend Wendy.

1

Wendy	Are you going out with Chuck tonight?
Laura	Uh-huh. I'm supposed to meet him at seven. What time is it now?
Wendy	Six-thirty.
Laura	You're kidding! I'd better get ready.
Wendy	Where are you going?
Laura	We haven't made up our minds yet. Maybe to a restaurant, maybe to a movie first.
Wendy	Why don't you go see *Citizen Kane* at the Classic Film Festival? It's supposed to be fantastic.
Laura	Oh, maybe we will. *Psycho* is also playing. I've heard it's really good too.
Wendy	If you like horror movies with lots of blood. Personally, I don't. Well, I really should be going. Do you want to go shopping tomorrow?
Laura	I'd like to, but I might have to go to the studio and do some work. Can I let you know first thing in the morning?
Wendy	Sure. That'll be fine. (*Rrring, rrring*)
Laura	Oh, there's the phone. It must be Chuck.
Wendy	Well, I'd better go then. Have a good time tonight.
Laura	Thanks. I'll talk to you tomorrow.

2. Figure it out

Say *True*, *False*, or *It doesn't say*.

1. Laura and Chuck might go to a restaurant.
2. Wendy has already seen *Citizen Kane*.
3. Wendy and Laura are thinking of going shopping tomorrow.
4. Laura is going to work tomorrow.
5. Laura hasn't seen *Psycho*.
6. Wendy will probably go to see *Psycho*.

3. Listen in

Laura is talking on the phone with Chuck. Read the statement below. Then listen to Laura's side of the conversation and choose *a*, *b*, or *c*.

Laura and Chuck are talking about _____ .

    a. a restaurant
    b. a class
    c. an Italian movie

21. Your turn

Work in groups. Read the poster about the Classic Film Festival. Then discuss these questions:

1. Have you ever seen any of the movies on the poster?
2. Do you like old movies? Why or why not?
3. What kinds of movies do you like the most? Why?
4. Is there a movie that most of the people in your group have seen? What did you think of the movie?

CLASSIC FILM FESTIVAL

LA DOLCE VITA
(1960)

In Federico Fellini's satire, a journalist enjoys the "sweet life" of Rome's high society, but is disturbed by it at the same time.

PSYCHO
(1960)

Alfred Hitchcock directed this thriller of murder and horror in a lonely country motel. This movie will have you on the edge of your seat.

CITIZEN KANE
(1941)

When a powerful newspaper publisher dies, a reporter tries to find out what kind of person he really was. Orson Welles both directed and starred in this brilliant piece of cinema.

RASHOMON (1951)

A crime is committed in eleventh-century Japan and is told from four different points of view. What *really* happened? This Academy Award-winning film by Akira Kurosawa brought Japanese cinema to the Western world.

How to say it

Practice the words. Then practice the conversations.

haven't [hǽvnt]　　hasn't [hǽznt]　　doesn't [dʌ́znt]　　didn't [dídnt]

A I haven't seen the Picasso exhibit yet.
B George hasn't either. Why don't you go with him?
A He doesn't want to see it.

A I didn't have time for lunch today.
B I didn't either.

22. 🔊

Film Directors For All Time

Name: FEDERICO FELLINI
Place of Birth: Rimini, Italy
Famous Films: *La Strada (1954)*
La Dolce Vita (1960)
Amarcord (1974)

When Fellini was a young boy, he ran away to join the circus. Even though he had to return to school, the experience greatly influenced his films, many of which are autobiographical. Fellini is known for combining realism and fantasy, often making up the story as he goes along.

Name: ALFRED HITCHCOCK
Place of Birth: London, England
Famous Films: *The Thirty-Nine Steps (1935)*
Notorious (1946)
Psycho (1960)

Hitchcock, the "Master of Suspense," made movies in both England and the United States. Many of them are about innocent people who get into trouble and can't seem to escape. Hitchcock used sound and camera techniques to heighten the feeling of panic. Many viewers enjoy trying to "spot" his short cameo appearances in all of his movies.

Name: AKIRA KUROSAWA
Place of Birth: Tokyo, Japan
Famous Films: *Rashomon (1950)*
Seven Samurai (1954)
Ran (1985)

Kurosawa was the first Japanese film director to become known throughout the world. His films mix together the old and the new, East and West. Kurosawa's film, *Ran*, a Japanese version of Shakespeare's *King Lear*, shows the influence of Western literature. Kurosawa has even been influenced by Hollywood Westerns.

Name: ORSON WELLES
Place of Birth: Kenosha, Wisconsin, U.S.A.
Famous Films: *Citizen Kane (1941)*
The Lady from Shanghai (1948)
Touch of Evil (1958)

Welles made his first and most influential film, *Citizen Kane*, when he was only 25. Considered by some film historians to be the greatest movie ever made, it is famous for unusual sound and camera techniques. Welles often acted in other directors' movies to raise money for films he wanted to direct, including a movie version of Shakespeare's *Othello*.

1. Read the article. Then scan it to find:

1. two directors known for their sound and camera techniques.
2. two directors who made films of plays by Shakespeare.
3. a director who made autobiographical films.

2. Match to make sentences.

1. Hitchcock always
2. Welles frequently
3. When Fellini was a child, he
4. Kurosawa was

a. appeared briefly in his own movies.
b. acted in movies directed by other people.
c. influenced by Hollywood Westerns.
d. left home to follow a traveling circus.

PREVIEW

FUNCTIONS/THEMES	LANGUAGE	FORMS
Talk about foreign languages	What languages do you speak? Which one do you speak the best? Do you speak English well? I hardly have an accent at all, but my grammar isn't very good.	*What* vs. *which* Adverbs
Talk about your family	Was either of your parents born in another country? They were both born here. Does she still speak Polish? She used to, but she doesn't anymore.	*Still* and *not . . . anymore*
Talk about events in the past	She's been here since she was six. He didn't know much English before he went to Canada.	Time clauses in the past: *when, before, after, as soon as,* and *since*
Tell how you met someone	How did you and your wife meet? I was teaching English at the time, and she was one of my students.	The past continuous

Preview the conversations.

1. Read the article. What are the main reasons people have immigrated to the United States?

2. Are there immigrants in your country? If so, discuss these questions with a partner:
   a. Where are they from?
   b. How long have they been in your country?
   c. Why did they come?
   d. What languages do they speak?

3. Have you ever lived in a different country (not your own)? Why did you choose to live there? Was it difficult to learn the language?

Immigration to the U.S.

Most U.S. citizens are either immigrants or descendants of immigrants. More than sixty million (60,000,000) people have left the countries of their birth and come to the United States to live. Some came for excitement and adventure. Others came to escape poverty and hunger, or political and religious oppression. Still others were brought over from Africa as slaves. These immigrants have brought their customs, languages, and foods, and have made the United States a country of great racial and ethnic diversity.

The original inhabitants of the United States were the Native American Indians. Today they make up less than 1 percent of the population.

23. What does the "K" stand for?

Luke Taylor and Maya Winston, two English teachers, are talking about their families.

A

Luke What an unusual necklace! What does the "K" stand for?
Maya "Koziol." It's my maiden name.
Luke Oh, that's Polish, isn't it?
Maya Yes. How did you know?
Luke My wife is Polish, and I've spent some time in Poland.
Maya Oh, is that where you met?
Luke No, actually, we met here in the States. I was teaching English at the time, and she was one of my students.

B

Maya Which language do you speak at home, English or Polish?
Luke English, most of the time. We used to speak more Polish before Stenia learned English so well.
Maya She had a good teacher.
Luke Well, she worked hard. In fact, she was one of my best students. She's also really good at languages.
Maya What languages does she speak?
Luke Polish, Russian, French, and English. She speaks English almost perfectly now. She still has a very slight accent, but you can hardly tell she's foreign.

C

Luke Was either of your parents born in Poland?
Maya Yes. They both were.
Luke Do they still speak Polish?
Maya My father used to, but he doesn't anymore. He
hasn't spoken it since my grandparents died. My
mother doesn't speak a word.
Luke How long has she been in this country?
Maya Since she was six. When she got here, she spoke
Polish, Russian, and German fluently. Unfortunately,
she forgot all of them as soon as she learned English.
Luke Do any of your relatives still live in Poland?
Maya No. They all live here now. Most of them came
over soon after my mother.

Figure it out

**1. Listen to the conversations. Then choose
a, b,** or **c.**

1. a. Stenia and Luke met in Poland.
   b. Stenia and Luke met in Russia.
   c. Stenia and Luke met in the U.S.

2. a. Luke and Stenia never speak Polish at home.
   b. Luke and Stenia sometimes speak Polish
      at home.
   c. Luke and Stenia always speak Polish at home.

3. Match the words in italics with their meaning.

1. She worked *hard*.
2. Do they *still* speak Polish?
3. *Actually*, we met here.
4. *As soon as* she learned English, she forgot Polish.
5. She *hardly* speaks Polish.
6. He *used* to speak Polish, but he doesn't anymore.
7. *Unfortunately*, she's forgotten Polish.
8. We speak English *most of the time*.

2. Listen again and say *True, False,* **or**
It doesn't say.

1. Koziol was Maya's name before she got married.
2. Stenia didn't know any English when she got to
   the U.S.
3. Stenia's grammar is excellent, but her accent
   is bad.
4. Maya's father still speaks Polish sometimes.
5. Maya's grandparents died a long time ago.

a. It's too bad.
b. in the past
c. almost always
d. now
e. a lot
f. very little
g. immediately after
h. as a matter of fact

24. What languages do you speak?

▶ **Listen to the job interview. Check (√) the languages the applicant says she can speak.**

____ Chinese ____ English ____ French
____ Italian ____ Russian ____ Spanish

▶ **Listen to the conversation.**
▶ **Interview three classmates. Have similar conversations, using your own information.**

A What languages do you speak?
B French, Spanish, and English.
A Which one do you speak the best?
B French.

Two languages: Which one do you speak *better*?

Three or more languages: Which one do you speak *the best*?

▶ **Study the frame: What vs. which**

What	languages	do you speak?
Which	language one	do you speak the best?

Use *which* instead of *what* when referring to a definite group of alternatives:
What languages (of all languages) do you speak ?
Which language (of the ones that you speak) do you speak the best?

▶ **Complete the conversations with *what* or *which*.**
▶ **Listen to check your work.**

I think I'll have soup. *What* kinds do you have?

Onion and pea soup. _____ one would you like?

Onion, please.

Excuse me— _____ way is the post office?

That way.

And _____ time does it close?

5:00 P.M.

_____ sports do you like?

I like *all* sports.

Yes, but _____ ones do you like the best?

Soccer and tennis.

1   2   3

► **Listen to the conversation.**
► **Act out a similar conversation with a partner.**

A Do you speak English well?
B I hardly have an accent at all, but my grammar isn't very good.

Do you speak English well?

I speak it very well. (It's my native language.)

I speak it fluently, but I make some mistakes.

I speak it correctly but slowly.

I speak it very fast, but my accent is terrible.

I understand it fairly well, but I speak it poorly.

I speak it very badly.

I work very hard. = I do a lot of work.
I hardly work at all. = I do almost no work.
I hardly have an accent at all. = I have almost no accent.

Do you speak French well?

► **Study the frame: Adverbs**

Adjectives	Adverbs
correct	correctly
perfect	perfectly
terrible	terribly
easy	easily
fantastic	fantastically
slow	slow/slowly
fast	fast
hard	hard
good	well

To form most adverbs, add *ly* to the adjective.
If the adjective ends in *le*, change the *e* to *y*.
If it ends in *y*, change the *y* to *i* and add *ly*.
If it ends in *c*, add *ally*.

► **Rewrite the sentences evaluating these students. Use adverbs instead of adjectives.**

Donna speaks French very well.

► **Write sentences evaluating your English ability, like the ones in exercise 7. Then compare your sentences with a partner.**

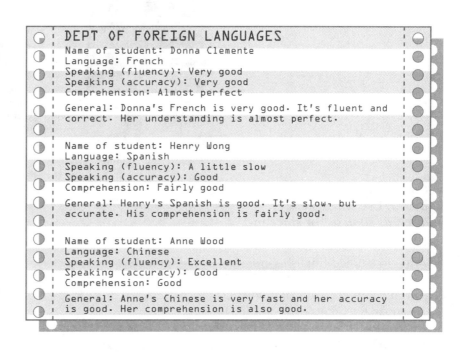

DEPT OF FOREIGN LANGUAGES
Name of student: Donna Clemente
Language: French
Speaking (fluency): Very good
Speaking (accuracy): Very good
Comprehension: Almost perfect

General: Donna's French is very good. It's fluent and correct. Her understanding is almost perfect.

Name of student: Henry Wong
Language: Spanish
Speaking (fluency): A little slow
Speaking (accuracy): Good
Comprehension: Fairly good

General: Henry's Spanish is good. It's slow, but accurate. His comprehension is fairly good.

Name of student: Anne Wood
Language: Chinese
Speaking (fluency): Excellent
Speaking (accuracy): Good
Comprehension: Good

General: Anne's Chinese is very fast and her accuracy is good. Her comprehension is also good.

25. Does she still speak Polish?

1 ► Listen to the three possible conversations.
► Work with a partner. Act out similar conversations about your relatives.

A Was either of your parents born in another country?

B Yes, my mother was. She was born in Poland.
A Does she still speak Polish?
B She used to, but she doesn't anymore.
A How long has she been in this country?
B Since she was six years old.

B Yes, both of them. They were born in Poland.

B No. They were both born here.

> Does she still speak Polish?
>
> Yes. She speaks it most of the time.
> Not a word. Unfortunately, she's forgotten it completely.
> No, not anymore. As soon as she came here, she stopped speaking it.

2 ► Study the frame: Time clauses in the past

I hardly **spoke** any English	**before**	I came here.
She **stopped** speaking it	**as soon as**	she arrived.
He **learned** English	**when**	he came here.
She **forgot** how to speak it	**after**	she got here.
She's **been** here	**since**	she was six.

Use the present perfect with *since.*

3 ► Antonio Freitas is an immigrant to Canada. Listen as he talks about himself.

ANTONIO FREITAS

I studied English in Brazil, but unfortunately, I didn't study very hard. So when I went to Canada at the age of twenty-five, I hardly spoke any English at all.

At first I lived with other Brazilians and spoke Portuguese most of the time. One day I was doing my laundry and I needed change. The only person in the laundromat was a young Canadian woman. When I spoke to her in my broken English, she answered me in Portuguese. She was studying it at college.

Well, it was love at first sight. We got married two years later, and we've done our laundry together ever since. Now I speak English much better—almost as well as my five-year-old son.

► Complete the sentences below. Use *when, before, after, as soon as,* or *since* in your answers.

1. Antonio studied English *before he went to Canada* .
2. He didn't know much English _____ .
3. Antonio and his wife fell in love _____ .
4. He spoke Portuguese most of the time _____ .
5. He and his wife got married two years _____ .
6. Antonio has been in Canada _____ .

26. How did you meet?

1 ▶ Listen to four people talk about how they met someone else. Match each conversation with the picture it describes.

2 ▶ Listen to the conversation.
▶ Act out similar conversations with a partner.

A How did you and your wife meet?
B I was teaching English, and she was one of my students.

> She *was* teaching English.
> We *were* taking the same course.

3 ▶ Study the frames: The past continuous

I He She	**was**		
		teaching	English.
We You They	**were**		

Form past continuous negative statements, yes-no questions, and information questions the same way as for the present continuous, but use a past tense form of be:
  I **wasn't watching** TV.
  Were you **eating** dinner?
  What **were** you **doing**?

4 ▶ Complete the conversations using the simple past tense or past continuous of the verbs in parentheses.
▶ Listen to check your work.

1. **A** How did you meet your best friend?
   B I _____ (take) a course at the university, and she _____ (be) in my class.

2. **A** How did you meet your husband?
   B Both of us _____ (stand) in line for movie tickets, and we _____ (strike up) a conversation.

3. **A** How did you get that sunburn?
   B I was _____ (lie) on the beach, and I _____ (fall) asleep!

4. **A** How did you get interested in Japanese art?
   B I (live) _____ in Japan, and a friend _____ (introduce) me to it.

5. **A** How did you miss your plane?
   B Well, I _____ (talk) on the phone, and I _____ (not/hear) them announce the flight.

6. **A** How did you get that ugly stain on your shirt?
   B Oh, I (eat) _____ an ice cream cone, and it _____ (drip) all over!

27. I guess my mind was somewhere else.

 Laura and Chuck are getting a bite to eat after seeing a movie.

1

Laura What a great movie! Wasn't it funny when he forgot her name?

Chuck Hmmm . . . I don't remember that part.

Laura It was one of the funniest parts of the movie!

Chuck I guess my mind was somewhere else.

Laura You were thinking about the interview again, weren't you?

Chuck I just can't seem to get it out of my mind. I really want that job, Laura.

Laura I know you do.

Chuck Mr. Dow seemed to think I was qualified. I can't figure out why I haven't heard yet. It's been nearly two weeks since I had the interview.

Laura Well, they said it would be about ten days. Listen, if you're so anxious to find out, why don't you call them and ask if they've made a decision yet?

Chuck Oh, I'm sure they'll let everyone know as soon as they've decided.

Laura Well, relax then. Let's think about what we're going to order. What's good here?

Chuck They used to have this great onion soup, but I don't see it anywhere on the menu.

Laura Maybe they don't serve it anymore. Here comes the waiter. Let's ask him.

2. Figure it out

Say *True, False,* or *It doesn't say.*

1. Chuck had a job interview almost two weeks ago.
2. Someone else got the job.
3. Chuck watched the movie very carefully.
4. Laura enjoyed the movie.
5. Chuck is unemployed.
6. Chuck has been to the restaurant before.

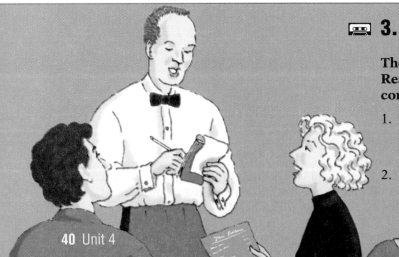

3. Listen in

The waiter is taking Laura and Chuck's order. Read the statements below. Then listen to the conversation and choose *a* or *b*.

1. The restaurant might be out of _____ .
   a. onion soup
   b. chicken soup

2. The last time Chuck ate at the restaurant _____ .
   a. the waiter was already working there
   b. the waiter wasn't working there yet

28. Your turn

The Karras family immigrated to the United States from Greece many years ago. Here's a page from their scrapbook. When do you think these photographs were taken? What do you think has happened to the family during the five generations shown in these pictures? Work in groups and make up a history of the Karras family.

Nicholas Karras and his youngest son, George, In Athens, Greece, a year before the family moved to the U.S.

The Karras brothers in the U.S.: Nicholas Jr., Gus, and George.

Helen Karras, daughter of George, is the first Karras to graduate from college.

Helen and her daughter, Christina.

Christina, her husband Alex, and their daughter Anna.

Anna visiting Athens, Greece.

How to say it

Practice the phrases. Then practice the conversation.

both of them [bóθəvəm]   some of them [sʌ́məvəm]   all of them [ɔ́ləvəm]

A Do your parents speak Greek?
B Yes, both of them do. They were born in Greece.
A What about your brothers and sisters?
B Some of them speak Greek to my parents, but all of them speak English very well too.

29.

THE FIRST AMERICANS

When did the first immigrants reach America? Scientists disagree on the date, but some say it may be much earlier than anyone thought.

The original Americans, called "Indians" by Columbus, were the descendants of immigrants. Do you know where they came from and when they first arrived in the Americas?

When Columbus "discovered" America in 1492, he found people already living there. Thinking he had landed in the East Indies, he called these people "Indians." But *they* didn't call themselves "Indians." Stretching from the top of North America to the tip of South America were many different groups, each with its own name and way of life.

Many scientists believe that the ancestors of these people migrated to America from Asia about 11,500 years ago. At the time, the northern half of the earth was covered in ice; a lot of the land that is now under water, was then dry land. Experts believe that people from Siberia followed the animals that they hunted and traveled to Alaska over land that is now a 50-mile body of water called the Bering Strait.

When did these people migrate to the New World? This is a difficult question to answer exactly. Archeologists look for clues in the earth by digging for the remains of these early peoples. Along with bones from humans and animals, they uncover pieces of pottery, tools, and even the remains of campfires. Then they use a special technique, called radiocarbon dating, to figure out the age of these artifacts by measuring the amount of radioactive carbon in them.

Recently, archeologists have discovered clues at digs in both North and South America that lead them to believe that humans first migrated to the New World not 11,500 years ago, but much earlier—20,000 or even 50,000 years ago. These discoveries are causing a lot of excitement and controversy among experts. Two of the most interesting sites are in Chile and Brazil.

In Monte Verde, Chile, scientists working at a dig found well-preserved artifacts including stone tools and wooden bowls. They also found a human footprint and the remains of a dwelling that is very similar to a type found in Siberia. Scientists estimate that humans lived in this place 12,500 years ago. Archeologists are now working on another site that may be almost 33,000 years old.

Most of the controversy about early settlements is over the site uncovered in Pedra Furada, Brazil. Archeologist Niéde Guidon found cave paintings dating back 12,000 years. But she also uncovered charcoal from old campfires and stone tools that she believes are at least 30,000 and maybe more than 50,000 years old. Radiocarbon testing supports her findings, but some scientists still have doubts. They say that the charcoal could be from general fires in the area and not from campfires, and the "tools" could be pieces of naturally formed rock. Guidon defends her findings and even comes up with a new idea of how the early settlers got to America—they may have traveled directly from Asia to South America in boats.

What will be uncovered next? Only time will tell . . .

EARLY AMERICAN SITES AND MIGRATION ROUTES

Land Route ———

Bering Land Bridge

Greenland ice Sheet

Pedra Furada, Brazil

Monte Verde, Chile

---

1. Read the article. Then match these words with their definitions.

1. remains	a. house or other place where people live
2. artifacts	b. sites being explored by archeologists
3. digs	c. tools or other objects made by humans
4. dwelling	d. people who come to live permanently in a new place
5. settlers	e. parts of something that are left after most of it has been destroyed

2. Discuss these questions.

1. Where did the first American immigrants come from?
2. Why is there so much disagreement about early settlements at the site at Pedra Furada?
3. Give two possible theories about how the first settlers got to America.

Review of units 1-4

1
► Debbie, Brian, and Jenny are guests at Meg and Jim's wedding reception in Boston. Complete Debbie's part of the conversation.
► Work in groups of three. Act out similar conversations.

Debbie _____
Brian Oh, hi, Debbie. Nice to see you, too. I hear you just got back from San Francisco.
Debbie _____
Brian No, but I'd like to go there. Everyone says it's a beautiful city. By the way, have you met Jenny?
Debbie _____
Brian Debbie, this is Jenny. Jenny's from Denver.
Debbie _____
Jenny Nice to meet you, too.
Debbie _____
Jenny I'm a photographer.
Debbie _____
Jenny Well, I used to work for a magazine, but I just opened my own studio.
Debbie _____
Jenny I just met Jim today, but I've known Meg since we were in college. We were both studying fine arts and we got to be friends.

2
► Imagine you're at the wedding reception. Strike up a conversation with someone you know. Use one of the sentences below or your own information. Keep the conversation going.

I hear you got a new job.　　*I hear you just got back from . . .*
I hear you're planning to . . .　*I hear you started your own business.*

3
► Work with a partner. You are both guests at the wedding. Play these roles.

Student A: You live in Boston. Find out how Student B knows Meg and Jim and if Student B has been to Boston before. If not, invite him or her to go sightseeing tomorrow.

Student B: Answer Student A's questions. You're a friend of Jim's. You've never been to Boston before, and you'll be there for two more days. You'd like to go sightseeing, but you might be busy tomorrow with friends.

4
► Meg, the bride, is dancing with her uncle at the reception. Listen to their conversation and say *True* or *False*.

1. Meg's uncle hasn't met Jim yet.
2. Meg and Jim went to the same university.
3. Meg works for an eye doctor now.

▶ Here are some other conversations taking place at the reception. Work with a partner. Say each conversation in a different way, using the words in parentheses.

1. **A** Do you two know each other? (met)
   B No, I don't believe we've met. (have)
   A *Have you two met?*
   B *No, I don't believe we have.*

2. **A** When did meet Meg? (How long)
   B Two years ago. (for)

3. **A** How long have you lived here? (always)
   B Since I was five. Before that I lived in Korea. (used to)

4. **A** Have you known Jim long? (When)
   B I've known him since we were in college. (met)

5. **A** Have you visited Hong Kong? (ever been)
   B No, but people say it's an exciting city. (heard)

6. **A** Have you always lived in Boston? (a long time)
   B No, I've only lived here for a month. (moved)

▶ Imagine you're at the wedding reception. Strike up a conversation with someone you don't know. Use one of the sentences in the box or your own ideas. Keep the conversation going.

> That's an interesting necklace.
> Are you from Boston?
> How do you know Meg and Jim?
> Have you tried these appetizers?
>   They're delicious.

▶ Jenny is in her hotel room in Boston after the reception. She's calling Phil, an old friend. Complete her conversation with the words in parentheses. Use the present perfect or the simple past tense.
▶ Listen to check your work.

. . . Hi, Phil! This is Jenny. I'm here in Boston. . . . I _____ (be) here for two days. . . . I _____ (get) here on Friday. . . . Well, yesterday I _____ (see) the Salvador Dalí exhibit at the Museum of Fine Arts, and today I _____ (go) to a wedding. . . . Meg Wilson and Jim Harris . . . . No, I don't think you know them. Meg and I _____ (go) to college together. . . . No, I _____ (not/see) Beth yet, but I just _____ (speak) to her on the phone a few minutes ago. We're thinking of getting together tomorrow night. Maybe you'd like to join us. . . . We _____ (not/decide) yet. . . . Oh, I _____ (already/see) it . . . . That's a good idea. I _____ (not/be) to the theater for months . . . . I'll call Beth back and ask her if she wants to see it. . . .

▶ **Beth is talking on the phone with Jenny. Which play are they talking about? Listen to Beth's side of the conversation and circle the ad.**

WAITING FOR SUMMER
by Michael Jeffreys
WILBUR THEATER
Monday–Saturday
8:00 p.m.

Lisa Stone and Keith Bolin in
The White Rose
Charles Street Theater
Tuesday–Saturday
8:00 p.m.

THAT WONDERFUL NIGHT
starring Elizabeth Hudson
Orpheum Theater
Monday–Saturday, 7:30 p.m.

▶ **A friend calls and asks if you'd like to see the play *Waiting for Summer* on Saturday night. Choose one of the roles below and act out the conversation with a partner.**

Role A: You've never heard of the play. At first you're not sure you can go because you have an exam on Monday, but you want to do something interesting this weekend.
Role B: You've heard that the play is really good, but you might not be free on Saturday night. Give a reason why you might be busy.
Role C: You've already seen the play. Suggest doing something else.

▶ **Jenny and Beth are waiting for Phil in front of the theater. Complete Beth's part of the conversation.**

Beth _____

Jenny No. I don't work for the magazine anymore. I have my own studio now.

Beth _____

Jenny For about a month. I'm really excited about it. I've always wanted to have my own business. But tell me, what's new with you?

Beth _____

Jenny Really? How did you meet him?

Beth _____

Jenny Was he born in Italy?

Beth _____

Jenny Since high school, huh? Does he still speak Italian?

Beth _____

Jenny No kidding. *You* speak Italian? Do you speak it well?

Beth _____

▶ **Imagine you're talking to a friend you haven't seen for a long time. Talk about your family, your job, things you've done, or people you've met.**

12 ▶ It's the day after Phil went to the theater with Jenny and Beth. He's talking to his friend Lou. Put the conversation in order.
▶ Listen to check your work.
▶ Act out a similar conversation with a partner.

___ Oh, I haven't seen it, but I've heard it's very good. How did you like it?

___ I've always wanted to see one of his plays. Where's it playing?

___ Well, maybe I'll go this weekend. I might ask Marilyn to go.

_1_ Have you seen any good movies lately?

___ Oh, she's already seen it. I saw her at the theater last night.

___ No, but I just saw a play last night—*Waiting for Summer.*

___ It was excellent. Michael Jeffreys wrote it, you know.

___ At the Wilbur Theater.

13 ▶ Work with a partner. Tell your partner about a movie, play, or some other event you went to recently. Answer your partner's questions.

14 ▶ Work with the same partner. Talk about your plans for next weekend.
▶ Say what you might and might not do. Then report to the class.

Lily might ride her motorcycle.
Boris might go for a midnight swim.

15 ▶ Listen to the first part of each conversation and choose the best response.

1. a. Nice to meet you, too.
   b. Nice to see you, too.

2. a. Thanks, it's from Greece.
   b. Oh, thanks.

3. a. No, I never have.
   b. Yes, I'm going next year.

4. a. Last year.
   b. For a year.

5. a. Six months ago.
   b. For six months.

6. a. She's fine.
   b. They're both fine.

7. a. Thanks, but I've already seen it.
   b. Thanks, but I've already read it.

8. a. Where does the other one live?
   b. Where do the other ones live?

9. a. No, not anymore.
   b. No, not yet.

10. a. Yes, he speaks it poorly.
    b. Yes, he speaks it fluently.

PREVIEW

FUNCTIONS/THEMES	LANGUAGE	FORMS
Ask for advice	Do you know of any hotels around here? Did you have anything special in mind? Just someplace clean and inexpensive. Which one is the nicest? The Harvest is the nicest, but it's also the most expensive.	Indefinite compounds with adjectives The superlative of adjectives
Ask how to get somewhere	What's the best way to get to The Harvest? You can either walk or take a bus. It's about a thirty-minute walk or fifteen minutes by bus. So, it's faster by bus.	Comparatives vs. superlatives
Ask for and give directions	Could you please tell me how to get to Toby's "Good Eats"? When you get to Yorkville, turn left. Stay on Bellair until you get to Bloor Street. You can't miss it.	Future time clauses with the simple present tense: *when, just before, just after, as soon as,* and *until*

Preview the conversations.

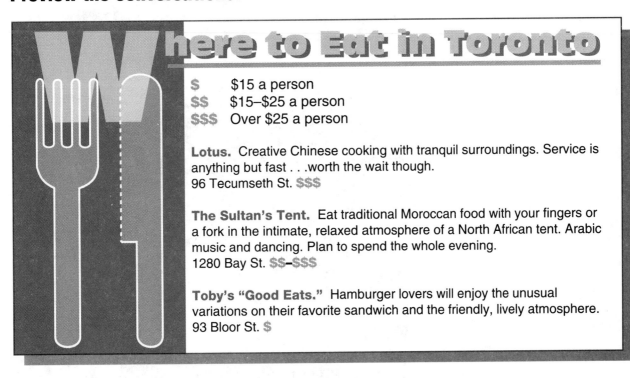

Where to Eat in Toronto

$ $15 a person
$$ $15–$25 a person
$$$ Over $25 a person

Lotus. Creative Chinese cooking with tranquil surroundings. Service is anything but fast . . .worth the wait though.
96 Tecumseth St. $$$

The Sultan's Tent. Eat traditional Moroccan food with your fingers or a fork in the intimate, relaxed atmosphere of a North African tent. Arabic music and dancing. Plan to spend the whole evening.
1280 Bay St. $$–$$$

Toby's "Good Eats." Hamburger lovers will enjoy the unusual variations on their favorite sandwich and the friendly, lively atmosphere.
93 Bloor St. $

1. Read the descriptions of three Toronto restaurants. Then choose a partner and compare the restaurants to each other. You may use these adjectives: *expensive, pricey, reasonable, cheap, relaxed, interesting,* and *lively.*
2. Now make plans with three other students to have dinner out in your town. Compare different restaurants and then decide where to go. Here are some more adjectives you may use: *close, far, small, large, crowded, romantic, exotic,* and *busy.*

30. You can't miss it.

Two tourists, Kathy and George Dupont, are looking for a place to have lunch in Toronto.

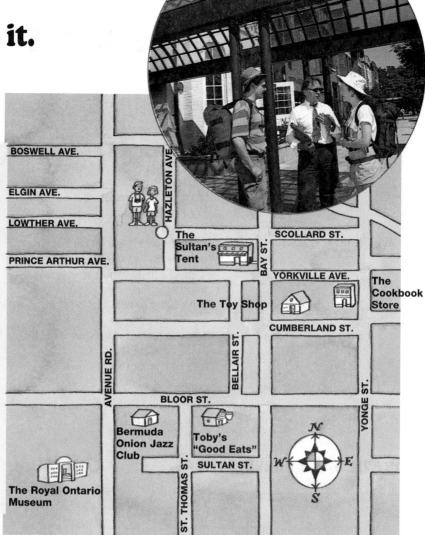

A

Kathy Excuse me. We're looking for a place to have lunch. Do you know of any restaurants around here?

Man in street Well, there are a lot of them. Did you have anything special in mind?

George Oh, just someplace reasonable with good food.

Man in street Well, you know, this is one of the most expensive areas in town.

Kathy Can you recommend a place that's not too expensive?

Man in street Let's see now. . . . The closest place that I can think of is Toby's. It's supposed to be reasonable, and everyone says the food is good. They serve all kinds of hamburgers.

George That sounds fine.

B

George Could you tell us how to get to the restaurant?

Man in street Do you know where Yorkville Avenue is?

George Yes.

Man in street Well, when you get to Yorkville, turn left. Then go one more block and turn right on Bellair. Just stay on Bellair until you get to Bloor Street. The restaurant will be right across the street. You can't miss it.

Kathy What's it called again?

Man in street Toby's "Good Eats."

Art Gallery of Ontar...

C

Kathy One more thing . . . what's the best way to get to the Art Gallery of Ontario?

Man in street You can either walk or take the subway.

George How far is it? My feet are killing me.

Man in street Oh, not that far. About a thirty-minute walk, I'd say.

George We'll take the subway.

Man in street Well, then after you eat, walk a couple of blocks west on Bloor and take the University subway south to St. Patrick.

Kathy Thanks a lot. You've been very helpful.

Man in street Don't mention it. Enjoy your day.

Figure it out

1. Listen to the conversation and choose the correct answer.

1. a. George and Kathy live in the neighborhood.
   b. George and Kathy don't know the neighborhood very well.

2. a. George and Kathy have walked a lot today.
   b. George and Kathy just got off the subway.

2. Listen again and say *True, False,* or *It doesn't say.*

1. George and Kathy don't want to spend a lot of money.
2. The man has eaten at Toby's many times.
3. George's feet hurt.
4. Most of the restaurants in the area are very reasonable.
5. George and Kathy are going to take the subway to the restaurant.

3. Choose *a* or *b*.

1. Do you know _____ ?
   a. where is Bloor Street
   b. where Bloor Street is

2. Could you tell us how _____ ?
   a. to get there
   b. do you get there

3. It's a _____ walk.
   a. ten-minutes
   b ten-minute

4. Stay on Bellair until _____ .
   a. you'll get to Bloor
   b. you get to Bloor

31. Do you know of any hotels around here?

1 ▶ **Read the three ads. Then listen to the conversation. Circle the ad for the hotel that the man describes.**

CONTINENTAL HOTEL
....
• swimming pool
• cable TV
• air conditioning
"One of the best values in the city."
740 Clark Street
555-2930

The Milburn Hotel
• Convenient location
• Reasonable rates
• Free parking

45 Bedford Avenue
555-9738

"In the heart of the city"
THE WESTGATE INN
Easy to reach by subway or bus
555-1925
273 Union Boulevard

2 ▶ **Listen to the three possible conversations.**
▶ **Work with a partner. Have similar conversations about restaurants and hotels in your town.**

A Do you know of any hotels around here?

B Yes. There's one on State Street.

B Well, there are quite a few. Did you have anything special in mind?
A No, nothing special. Just someplace clean and inexpensive.

B No. I'm afraid I don't.

a hotel	a restaurant
clean	reasonable
convenient	unusual
inexpensive	close
modern	with good food
with parking	with a nice atmosphere
	with fast service

3 ▶ **Study the frames: Indefinite compounds with adjectives**

someone	anyone	no one	everyone	**someone** important
something	anything	nothing	everything	**anywhere** interesting
someplace	anyplace	no place	everyplace	**nothing** special
somewhere	anywhere	nowhere	everywhere	**everything** good

Did you do *anything special?*

4 ▶ **Two roommates are talking. Complete the conversation with indefinite compounds followed by adjectives when appropriate.**
▶ **Listen to a possible conversation.**

A Hi! How was your day? Did you do *anything special*?
B No, _____ _____.
A Well, did you go _____?
B No, _____ _____.
A That's the TV section, isn't it? Is there _____ _____ on TV?
B _____ _____. Just the same old shows. I've already seen _____ _____.
A Oh, by the way, did _____ call?
B No, _____.

32. Which one is the nicest?

▶ **Bruce just moved into his apartment. Listen to the conversation with his neighbor, Jim, and check (√) the things they talk about.**

a restaurant   a doctor   a dentist   a shoe store   a department store   a bakery

▶ **Listen to the three possible conversations and practice them with a partner.**
▶ **Look at the pictures above and act out similar conversations about your neighborhood.**

A Can you recommend a nice restaurant in this neighborhood?

B Yes. I know of one.
A Is it expensive?
B No, not really.

B Well, there are three— The Harvest, The Kitchen, and Sylvia's.
A Which one is the nicest?
B The Harvest is the nicest, but it's also the most expensive.

B No, I'm sorry, I don't know of any.

> *Two* restaurants: The Harvest is *nicer than* The Kitchen.
> *Three or more* restaurants: The Harvest is *the nicest* restaurant.

▶ **Study the frames: The superlative of adjectives**

Sylvia's has		**fastest**	service in town.
The Harvest is	the	**most expensive**	restaurant.
The Kitchen is		**least expensive**	restaurant.
It's			**nicest**.

Some adjectives	Which one is . . .?
nice	the nicest
close	the closest
far	the farthest
good	the best
bad	the worst
expensive	the most expensive
inexpensive	the least expensive

▶ **Complete the conversation with the superlative form of the adjectives in parentheses.**
▶ **Listen to check your work.**

A I need a new pair of shoes. Can you recommend a good shoe store?
B Well, Shoe King is _____ (good), but it's also _____ (far).
A Do you know of one that's not too far?
B Let me see. _____ (close) place I can think of is Tip Top Shoes.
A Are their shoes expensive?
B Oh no. It's _____ (inexpensive) shoe store in town. They also have _____ (large) selection.
A That sounds fine. Thanks.

33. What's the best way to get to The Harvest?

▶ **Listen to the conversation.**
▶ **Work with a partner. Act out similar conversations about places in your town.**

A What's the best way to get to The Harvest?
B You can either walk or take a bus.
A How far is it?
B Oh, it's about a thirty-minute walk or fifteen minutes by bus.
A So, it's faster by bus.

Some means of transportation	Some times
walk	a thirty-minute walk
take a bus	a fifteen-minute bus (subway) ride
take a subway	ten minutes by subway (bus)
drive	a two-hour drive

thirty minutes, *but* a thirty-minute walk

▶ **Study the frames: Comparatives vs. superlatives**

Before adding *-er* or *-est*:

Drop the *e* when an adjective ends in *e* (*close-closer-closest*).
Double the consonant when an adjective ends in a single vowel + a consonant (*big - bigger - biggest*).
Change *y* to *i* (*busy - busier - busiest*).

Adjective	Comparative form	Superlative form
fast	fast**er**	**the** fast**est**
close	clos**er**	**the** clos**est**
big	big**ger**	**the** big**gest**
busy	bus**ier**	**the** bus**iest**
good	**better**	**the best**
bad	**worse**	**the worst**
far	far**ther**	**the** far**th**est
expensive	**more** expensive	**the most** expensive
inexpensive	**less** expensive	**the least** expensive

▶ **Complete the letter, using the comparative or superlative form of the adjectives in parentheses.**
▶ **Listen to check your work.**

> December 20th
>
> Dear Mary and Bob,
>
> I'm really sorry I haven't written, but the holidays are the _busiest_ (busy) time of the year for me at the store. The children are a lot _____ (big) than when you saw them. I think Nancy is going to be _____ (tall) one in the family very soon. Jim is one of _____ (good) students in his class. He had a little trouble with math last year, but it's a lot _____ (easy) for him now. Harry is _____ (happy) and _____ (relaxed) since he started his new job. _____ (important) thing is that the hours are _____ (short).
>
> This has been one of _____ (bad) winters in a long time. I hope the weather gets _____ (warm) soon.
>
> How's everything with you? Do you have plans to

▶ **Work with a partner. Find out: What is your partner's busiest day of the week? What was the happiest day of your partner's life? What was the most expensive thing your partner ever bought? What's the best book your partner ever read? What's the worst movie your partner has ever seen?**

34. When you get to Yorkville, turn left.

1 ▶ **Listen to the conversation and practice it with a partner.**

A Could you please tell me how to get to Toby's "Good Eats"?
B Sure. Do you know where Yorkville Avenue is?
A Yes, I do.
B Well, when you get to Yorkville, turn left. Then go one more block and turn right on Bellair. Stay on Bellair until you get to Bloor Street. Toby's will be right across the street. You can't miss it!
A Thanks a lot.
B Don't mention it.

Some places in Toronto
Toby's "Good Eats"
The Sultan's Tent
The Royal Ontario Museum
Bermuda Onion Jazz Club
The Toy Shop
The Cookbook Store

2 ▶ **Work with a partner. Imagine you're at the corner of Hazelton and Scollard in Toronto. Ask how to get to one of the places listed in the box. Your partner will give your directions using the map on page 48.**

Some locations
across the street
on the left
about halfway down the block
at/on the corner

3 ▶ **Study the frames: Future time clauses with** *when, just before, just after, as soon as,* **and** *until.*

Turn right You'll see the store	**when** **just before** **just after** **as soon as**	you get to Bloor.
Stay on Bellair	**until**	

Use a simple present tense verb in time clauses that refer to future time, even when another verb in the sentence is in the future:

Turn right when you get to Bloor.
You'll pass two traffic lights before you get there.

4 ▶ **Look at the map. Imagine you're walking on First Street and a driver asks you for directions to Mama's Kitchen. Complete the conversation with appropriate time clauses.**

Driver Excuse me. How do you get to Mama's Kitchen from here?
You Stay on First Street <u>until you get to</u> Market Street. _____ Market, turn right. Then go straight ahead _____ Baker Street. _____ Baker, you'll see a travel agency. _____ the travel agency, get in the left lane. Turn left on Baker at the light. Mama's Kitchen is near the end of the block on the left.

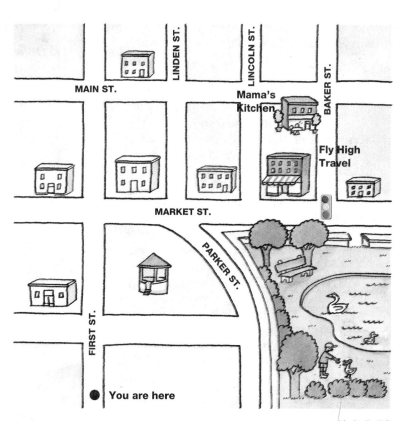

35. You can't keep them home anymore.

Laura's mother, Mrs. Enders, is shopping for a gift for Laura's sister at Lee's Housewares.

1

Mrs. Lee	May I help you find something, or are you just looking?
Mrs. Enders	I'm trying to find something for my daughter. She just moved into a new apartment.
Mrs. Lee	Did you have anything special in mind?
Mrs. Enders	Something practical. I know she needs a lot of things. . . . Maybe a nice pot.
Mrs. Lee	Well, these are the best pots we carry. Feel how heavy this one is.
Mrs. Enders	I'm afraid it's a bit too heavy. I have to carry it with me on the plane.
Mrs. Lee	Well, they also come in smaller sizes. I've had some for ten years, and they're still like new.
Mrs. Enders	I'll take this smaller one. Do you accept credit cards?
Mrs. Lee	No, I'm sorry, we don't. We take either cash or a check with ID. Where does your daughter live?
Mrs. Enders	In Chicago. In fact, both of my daughters live in Chicago. You know kids nowadays. You can't keep them home anymore.
Mrs. Lee	It's true. My son is thinking of moving to Chicago too, as a matter of fact. He had an interview there. Now he's waiting to hear if he got the job.
Mrs. Enders	Who do I make the check out to?
Mrs. Lee	Lee's Housewares.

2. Figure it out

Say *True*, *False*, or *It doesn't say.*

1. Mrs. Enders is going to Chicago.
2. Mrs. Lee's son is moving to Chicago.
3. Laura's sister is looking for an apartment.
4. Mrs. Enders buys the heaviest pot.
5. Mrs. Enders has two daughters.
6. Mrs. Enders gives Mrs. Lee cash.

3. Listen in

Mrs. Enders also needs a bathroom scale. Read the statement below. Then listen to the conversation and choose *a* or *b*.

Ace Hardware is _____ .
a. before The Shoe Place
b. after The Shoe Place

36. Your turn

Imagine that you live in Kyoto, Japan. Your partner is a tourist who starts a conversation with you and then asks you the questions below. Using the map, give your partner directions. You are standing on the corner of Nichioji and Shijo streets.

A *Where can I get a train to Tokyo?*
B *Walk about two blocks along Shijo Street and turn right on Horikawa Street. Then walk two blocks to Shichijo Street. The train station is on the left, near the corner of Horikawa and Shichijo.*

1. Where can I get some information about Kyoto?
2. Where can I buy some presents for my family?
3. I'd like to see a traditional Japanese play. Is there a theater near here?
4. I'd like to visit Kyoto University. Is it far from here?

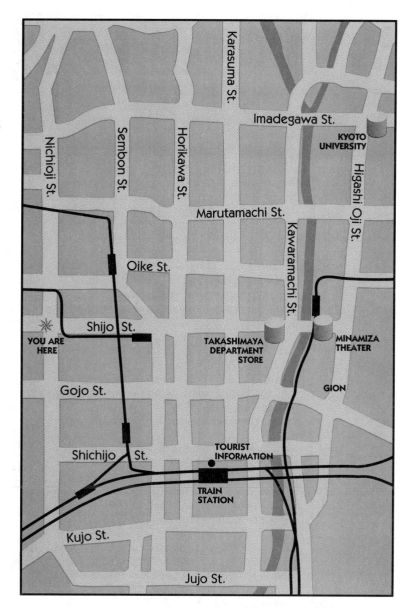

How to say it

Practice the conversation.

A How do I get to the train station from here?

B You can either drive or take a bus.

A Is it far?

B Well, it's about a ten-minute drive and about twenty minutes by bus.

Gion, the neigborhood of the Minamiza Theater

37.

When in Japan...

Do you know the customs in Japan for greeting other people? . . . eating a meal in a restaurant? . . . tipping? . . . giving gifts? Read the article and find out.

Do you enjoy traveling to other countries? Do you like to see new sights, taste new foods, and understand how foreign cultures are different from your own? There is a proverb that goes: When in Rome, do as the Romans do. This means that it is a good idea to try to learn the customs of the place you are visiting, and then behave in a similar fashion.

If you plan to travel to Japan, it might be helpful to know some Japanese customs about public behavior, dining out, tipping, and gifts before you go.

Even though you may be familiar with pictures of people in Tokyo crowded into trains during rush hour, be aware that people in Japan value their personal space. You might be used to touching someone on the arm or giving a pat on the shoulder, but do not do this in Japan. You greet a person by bowing or nodding, or sometimes by shaking hands. If you want to get the attention of a waiter or a salesperson, put your hand out in front of you, palm down, and wave it up and down. Don't confuse this with the gesture for "No," which is to wave your right hand back and forth in front of your face, with your palm facing left.

When dining out, before you start a meal, you will be given a basket with a hot towel in it. Use this towel to wipe your hands and then put it back in the basket. A napkin is not usually used. Be sure to wait until the older people at your table pick up their chopsticks before you begin eating.

You will find rice served at every meal. Always alternate a bite of rice with a bite of the side dishes. Don't eat just one dish at a time; this is considered rude. Drink soup directly from the bowl, but don't finish your soup before eating other dishes; it should accompany the entire meal.

When it is time to pay the bill, if the other person has invited you to dinner, let that person pay. If you wish to treat, be the first one to pick up the bill. Don't spend time checking over the bill. Honesty is very important and you can assume that the numbers are correct. And your change will not be counted out in front of you; it will just arrive on a tray. There is no need to leave a tip, for tipping is almost unheard of in Japan.

You will find that gifts are important. You should bring something when you visit, but it shouldn't be too expensive or your host will be uncomfortable. Avoid giving four of anything—the word for "four" is similar to the word for "death." All gifts, even money, should be wrapped, but your host will probably not open the gift in front of you, in order to show that the act of giving is more important than the actual gift. Use both hands when you give or receive a gift.

Remember, people always appreciate tourists who respect their customs. Happy traveling!

1. What advice would you give to a visitor to Japan about:

1. greeting or meeting someone for the first time.
2. eating in a restaurant.
3. paying the bill and tipping.
4. giving gifts.

2. How do these Japanese customs differ from customs in other countries you know?

FUNCTIONS/THEMES	LANGUAGE	FORMS
Express an obligation	I have to be at a meeting at noon. I'm supposed to pick up the kids at 5:00. I'd better go.	*Have to* and *be supposed to* *Had better* Two-word verbs
Leave a message with someone	If my son calls, tell him to be ready at six.	
Make a request	Could you explain them to me?	*Could*
Ask a favor of someone Offer to do someone a favor	Would you do me a favor? Would you please give this note to Mary for me? Would you explain this to me? Oh, I'll call her for you. I'll introduce you to him.	*Would* Indirect objects with *to* and *for* Direct and indirect objects
Ask for help	Could you show me how to work the VCR? I'm not sure how to record.	Question words with infinitives
Call an office	May I tell her who's calling? Would you have her call me when she gets back?	

Preview the conversations.

For __Ms. Clark__
Date __10/14__   Time __2:00__
WHILE YOU WERE OUT
M __r. John Willard__
From __The Wheaton Company__
Phone No. __555–3456__
☑ TELEPHONED
☑ PLEASE CALL   ☑ URGENT
☐ WILL CALL AGAIN   ☐ WANTS TO SEE YOU
☐ RETURNED YOUR CALL   ☐ CAME TO SEE YOU
Message __He'll be out from__
__2:30 to 3:00__

Read the message form. Then choose a partner and act out the conversations in the two situations below. Play the role of John Willard or Anne Jenkins. End the second conversation any way you wish.

1. John Willard calls Joan Clark, the president of Clark Associates, at 2:00 P.M. Ms. Clark is at a meeting. Her assistant, Anne Jenkins, takes the message on the message form.

2. At 4:30 P.M., Mr. Willard calls again because Ms. Clark hasn't called him back. Ms. Clark just got back, and Ms. Jenkins gave her the message as soon as she came in.

38. Do you know what time it is?

 It's a busy day for Anne Jenkins, an administrative assistant at Clark Associates.

A

Joan Anne, do you know what time it is?

Anne It's five to twelve.

Joan Listen, would you do me a favor? I have a lunch meeting with Alex Post, and I'm supposed to be there at noon. Would you call him for me and tell him I'm on my way?

Anne Sure.

Joan Thanks a lot. Oh, and one more thing . . . if my son Johnny calls, tell him to be ready at six. I'll pick him up on my way home.

Anne O.K.

Joan Oh, wait, I'd better call my husband. He might think *he's* supposed to pick up Johnny.

Anne Why don't you just go? I'll call him for you.

Joan Do you mind?

Anne No, not at all.

Joan Thanks so much. By the way, did you send Mr. Post our sales report?

Anne Yes. I sent it to him last week.

Joan I can always count on you, Anne. Well, I'm off. I should be back no later than three.

B

Receptionist Post, Cramden, and Lowe.

Anne Alex Post, please. (*Rrring, rrring*)

Mr. Post's assistant Mr. Post's office.

Anne May I speak to Mr. Post, please?

Mr. Post's assistant May I tell him who's calling?

Anne Yes, this is Anne Jenkins from Clark Associates.

C

Anne Good afternoon, Clark Associates.
Donald May I please speak to Ms. Clark?
Anne I'm sorry, she's not in the office.
Donald When do you expect her back?
Anne She should be back by three. Would you like to leave a message?
Donald This is Donald Todd. Would you please have her call me? My number is 555-4433. It's quite important.
Anne I'll give her the message as soon as she gets in.
Donald Thank you.
Office worker Uh . . . excuse me, can I ask you a question? Could you show me how to work the photocopier? I'm not sure where to put the paper.
Anne Sure, I'd be glad to.
Office worker Maybe you could explain the instructions to me. I can't seem to figure them out.

D

Joan Well, see you tomorrow.
Anne I'd better go, too. Thursday's my daughter's birthday, and I want to get her a new robe.
Joan I think you're going to have to buy it for her tomorrow. The stores are closing in fifteen minutes.
Anne Oh, no! You're right. I guess I lost track of the time.

Figure it out

1. Listen to the conversations. Then choose *a* or *b*.

1. a. Joan is going to pick up her son.
   b. Joan's husband is supposed to pick up their son.

2. a. Joan will be back at three.
   b. Joan expects to be back before three.

2. Listen again and say *True, False,* or *It doesn't say.*

1. Joan is going to be late for her meeting.
2. Joan's son might call.
3. Donald Todd called before three.
4. The office worker has used the photocopier before.
5. Anne has worked at Clark Associates for a long time.
6. Anne always knows what time it is.

3. Match.

1. Would you please have her
2. Tell my son
3. I gave it
4. I'm not sure where
5. I bought it
6. He explained
7. He asked

a. me that question.
b. for you.
c. call me.
d. to you.
e. that question to me.
f. to put the paper.
g. to call me.

39. I'm supposed to pick up the kids.

▶ **Rita just started a job as a receptionist. Her boss is explaining the job on the first day. Listen and check (√) Rita's responsibilities on the list.**

Both *I have to* and *I'm supposed to* show obligation, but *I'm supposed to* can also show that something was planned or arranged:

> I **have to** be at a meeting at noon. (So I'm going.)
> I'm **supposed to** be at a meeting now. (But I'm not there.)

▶ **Now use the checklist to talk about Rita's job. Use *has to* and *is supposed to*.**

Rita is supposed to be at work at 8:30 A.M.

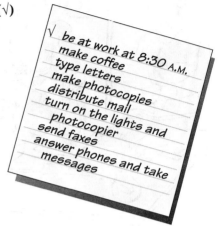

√ be at work at 8:30 A.M.
make coffee
type letters
make photocopies
distribute mail
turn on the lights and photocopier
send faxes
answer phones and take messages

▶ **Listen to the conversation.**
▶ **Act out similar conversations using the information in the appointment book.**

A Do you know what time it is?
B It's ten to five.
A Oh, I'd better go. I'm supposed to pick up my kids at 5:00.

When the object of a two-word verb is a noun, the verb can usually be separated or not separated:

Pick the kids **up**.   **Turn** the copier **on**.
Pick up the kids.   **Turn on** the copier.

When the object of a two-word verb is a pronoun (it, them, her, him, etc.) the verb must be separated:

Pick them **up**.
Turn it **on**.

MARCH 19

19 *MONDAY*

10:00 department meeting

12:00 meet Joe for lunch

3:00 call Henry Stone

5:00 pick up the kids

7:00 opera

▶ **Work with a partner. Talk about obligations you have today and tomorrow.**

I'm supposed to meet my sister at six.
I have to go the dentist tomorrow.

LEAVE A MESSAGE WITH SOMEONE

▶ **Joan Clark left messages with Anne Jenkins for these people. Match the people with the messages.**

a. Tell her I'll call her back after three.
b. Tell him to come fix the photocopier as soon as he can.
c. Tell her I'll pick up the airline tickets tomorrow.

the travel agent

the repairman

my mother

▶ **Work with a partner. Give your partner messages for people who might call you.**

If my sister calls, tell her to meet me at six.

40. Would you explain this to me?

1. ▶ What requests are these people making? Complete the conversations with the phrases in the box.
   ▶ Listen to check your work.
   ▶ Practice the conversations with a partner.

a. explain them to me
b. send it to him
c. give them back to her
d. introduce me to him

ASK A FAVOR OF SOMEONE • *WOULD* • INDIRECT OBJECTS WITH *TO* AND *FOR*

2. ▶ Look at the pictures and complete the conversations with the phrases in the box.
   ▶ Listen to check your work.
   ▶ Practice the conversations with a partner.

a. give this note to Mary for me
b. call a taxi for me
c. buy me a copy of *Time* on your way home
d. explain this math problem to me

3. ▶ Work with a partner. Ask him or her to do you a favor. Use your own ideas of the favors in the box below.

Some favors

Get a bottle of aspirin **for me** at the drugstore.
Buy a newspaper **for me** when you go out.
Make an appointment **for me** with Dr. Janik.

Lend your book **to me** when you're done with it.
Explain this problem **to me**.

41. Oh, I'll call her for you.

1 ▶ **Listen to the conversation and practice it with a partner.**

A I'd better call Nancy. She's expecting me in five minutes.
B Oh, I'll call her for you.

2 ▶ **Work with a partner. Look at the pictures and act out conversations like the one in exercise 1. Student A: Imagine you are the person in the picture. Student B: Offer to do Student A a favor.**

I'd better call the dentist and tell her I'm going to be late.

I'd better make some coffee or I'll fall asleep.

I'd better pick up some milk at the store. There's none left.

3 ▶ **Study the frames:**
Direct and indirect objects

	Direct object		Indirect object
Give	**the book**	to	**Joe**.
Buy	**it**	for	**him**.

	Indirect object	Direct object
Give	**Joe**	**the book**.
Buy	**him**	

Use *to* before the indirect object with these verbs:

bring	sell	take
give	send	tell
lend	show	

Use *for* before the indirect object with these verbs:

bake	find	save
build	get	
buy	make	

To + the indirect object always comes *after* the direct object of these verbs:

describe	explain	say
introduce	return	

Explain the instructions **to me**.

The indirect object always comes *before* the direct object of the verb *ask:*

He **asked me** a question.

4 ▶ **Complete the conversations, using direct and indirect object pronouns.**
▶ **Listen to check your work.**
▶ **Practice the conversations with a partner.**

1. **A** Your friend Pete looks interesting. I'd really like to meet ___*him*___.
   B Oh, I'll introduce __*you to him*__.

2. **A** I borrowed this book from Laila a month ago. I really should return _____.
   B She's in my class. I'll give _____.

3. **A** I've looked everywhere for my keys, but I can't find _____.
   B Take it easy. I'll find _____.

4. **A** This math problem is really hard. I don't understand _____.
   B Don't worry. I'll explain _____.

5 ▶ **Talk to your classmates. Tell them about things you'd better do or are having a problem with. Your classmates will offer to do you a favor.**

42. I'm not sure how to record.

ASK FOR HELP • QUESTION WORDS WITH INFINITIVES

1 **Listen to the conversation and practice it with a partner.**

A Excuse me. Could you show me how to work the VCR? I'm not sure how to record.
B Sure. I'd be glad to.
A And maybe you could explain this form to me. I don't know what to write on this line.
B I'm not sure what to write on it either.

2 ▶ **Study the frame: Question words with infinitives**

	Where do you put the paper? How do you turn on the machine?
I'm not sure I don't know	**where to put** the paper. **how to turn on** the machine.

3 ▶ **Work with a partner. Ask for help operating these machines. Act out conversations like the one in exercise 1.**

answering machine

coffee maker

photocopier

fax machine

CALL AN OFFICE

4 ▶ **Listen to the conversation and practice it with a partner.**

A May I speak to Ms. Clark, please?
B May I tell her who's calling?
A This is Jim Todd.
B One moment. (*Pause*) I'm sorry. She's not in her office.

A When do you expect her back?
B She should be back by three. Would you like to leave a message?
A Yes. Could you ask her to call me? My number is 555-4433.
B I'll give her the message as soon as she gets back, Mr. Todd.

5 ▶ **Work with a partner. Take turns playing these roles:**

Student A: Call Clark Associates and ask to speak to one of the people in the pictures.
Student B: Play the role of the receptionist. Use the information below the pictures.

Mr. Gray

Mr. Gray just stepped out for a few minutes.

Ms. Chu

Ms. Chu is on vacation until next Monday.

Mr. Benowitz

Mr. Benowitz is out to lunch until two.

Unit 6 **63**

43. I was starting to worry.

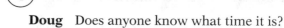 Back in Seattle, Washington, Doug is eating dinner with his family.

1

Doug	Does anyone know what time it is?
Mr. Lee	It's exactly seven o'clock.
Doug	I'd better get going soon. Someone's supposed to come over at eight to look at the apartment.
Mrs. Lee	Well, you can't leave before you have a piece of this cake Dad made.
Doug	Hey, chocolate cake! All right!
Mr. Lee	It's in honor of your new job.
Doug	You know, I still can't believe I got it. I was starting to worry when two weeks went by with no news.
Mr. Lee	Well, you know what they say, "No news is good news."
Doug	Hey, Ricky, how would you like to do your favorite brother a big favor? Could you and some of your friends give me a hand packing on Saturday?
Ricky	Sure, I guess so.
Doug	Thanks, Ricky. You're a great brother.

2. Listen in

Meanwhile in Chicago, Carlos, one of Laura's coworkers, gives her a telephone message. Read the statements below. Then listen to the conversation and choose *a* or *b*.

1. Chuck wants Laura _____ .
   a. to call him back
   b. to meet him after work

2. Laura is expecting Jack Thomson _____ .
   a. to call her
   b. to come to the office

3

(Laura dials Chuck's number.)

Chuck	Hello?
Laura	Hi, Chuck. You sound kind of depressed. Is anything wrong?
Chuck	Remember I was starting to worry when I hadn't heard anything in two weeks? Well, today I got a call. . . .

4. Figure it out

Say *True*, *False*, or *It doesn't say*.

1. Doug didn't get the new job.
2. Doug has already found an apartment in Chicago.
3. Doug is expecting someone at his apartment.
4. Ricky and his friends are going to help Doug.
5. Doug and Chuck probably applied for the same job.

44. Your turn

Work with a partner. Look at the pictures and try to figure out what each person's job is. Describe what each person has to do on a typical work day.

Discuss these questions in groups.

1. Of these six jobs, which one is the most interesting to you? The least interesting? Why?
2. Do you have a job? If so, describe what you do on a typical work day.

Here are some things people think about when they are looking for a job. In groups, discuss which of these would be most important to you. Can you add to the list?

- good salary and benefits
- independence: being your own boss
- physical activity

- excitement
- variety: doing many different things

- working with people
- travel
- working outdoors

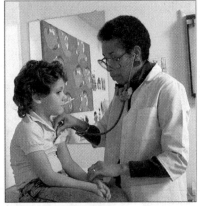

How to say it

Practice the phrases. Then practice the conversation.

| call her | [kɔ́lər] | ask him | [ǽskɪm] |
| called him | [kɔ́ldɪm] | tell him | [tɛl̆ɪm] |

A Bill is back from lunch.
B Anne Murphy called him before. Tell him to call her back right away. And ask him to call Beth Watson too.

45.

$ KNOW WHAT YOU'RE WORTH BEFORE YOU SEEK A RAISE $

Look at exercise 3 at the bottom of the page and write your answer to the last question: "What will you say?" After you've read the article, look at your answer again and see if you would change it in any way.

by Cynthia Hanson

Do you think you deserve a raise? Then ask for it.

In today's corporate climate, most regular salary hikes have shrunk or disappeared. Increasingly, employment experts say you'll have to ask if you want a pay boost.

"If you won't fight for what you're worth, what you're saying is 'I don't know if I have similar market value elsewhere,'" says Marilyn Moats Kennedy, a career counselor in Wilmette, Illinois.

Further, says John Leonard, a New York career management consultant, it's part of your job to make your case: "For you to get a raise, management has to think you're valuable. And no one will really know your brilliance unless you tell them."

Fearing that they'll be denied a raise, many people never request one. But experts say you'll gain respect if you make a strong case and deliver it in a professional manner.

How can you increase your chances? Experts offer these strategies:

- Do your homework. "You must know the industry standard for your job and where you fall on the salary scale at your company," Leonard says. Professional associations and coworkers are excellent sources.

- Think timing. If your boss submits annual budgets in September, request an appointment in July. Or take advantage of the success of an important assignment by seeking a raise after you've made a significant contribution.

- Quantify your accomplishments. To get a raise, you'll have to demonstrate how your performance contributes to the company's profits.

- Keep it career-focused. Whining about your salary will kill your chances for a raise. Steer the discussion to your contributions over the past year and your desire for career growth. And never threaten to quit. "When people say, 'Give me more money or I'll leave,' more often than not, the boss says, 'I wish you good luck,'" Leonard says.

- Rehearse. "You must come across as serious and prepared, not casual," Kennedy says. It's helpful to outline your achievements on paper, then practice delivering them aloud, either in front of a mirror, before a friend, or on a video.

- Know what you want. It's crucial to specify either a percentage increase or salary figure that should be in line with your market value and accomplishments. If you're turned down for an increase, ask for a reason and another review in six months. As a last resort, ask for alternatives such as more vacation time or the opportunity to attend training seminars. Both are likely to be easier to negotiate than a bigger paycheck.

- Follow-up. Regardless of the outcome, thank your boss for the meeting, either in a personal note or computer message. A healthy relationship with your boss is essential to your career growth and courtesy will keep it on track.

---

1. **Match the words from the article with the best meanings.**

   1. seek
   2. boost
   3. denied
   4. whining
   5. steer
   6. quantify
   7. come across as
   8. delivering
   9. last resort
   10. on track

   a. saying
   b. complaining
   c. appear to be
   d. measure
   e. final try
   f. working smoothly
   g. raise
   h. turned down for
   i. ask for
   j. direct

2. **What does "Do your homework" mean in this article? What is meant by the expression "I wish you good luck"?**

3. **Have you ever asked for a pay raise? Did you get it? Why or why not? Imagine you are going to ask for a pay raise. What will you say?**

FUNCTIONS/THEMES	LANGUAGE	FORMS
Talk about exercise Talk about likes and dislikes	Do you ever get any exercise? Do you like to swim? I ought to exercise more, but I can never seem to find the time. I've always enjoyed swimming. I hate getting up early on weekends.	Infinitives vs. gerunds
Talk about weight and height	Has he lost (a lot of) weight? Yeah. Twenty pounds. How tall is he? Five foot ten.	
Invite someone	I'm going biking with Bill and a friend of ours on Saturday. How about joining us?	Possessive pronouns and possessives of names
Ask where to get something	Do you know where I can rent a bike?	
Talk about your family	She's a lot like me. She's very different from me. Did you use to get along when you were younger? Not too well. We used to fight a lot.	The past with *used to*

Preview the conversations.

People are exercising more than ever before. A recent poll shows that more than 70 percent of the adult population exercises daily. Why?

- Because when you're in good physical shape, you look and feel better.
- Because vigorous exercise helps prevent illness and is important for weight control.

1. Read the paragraph about exercise. Then choose a partner and discuss these questions.

   a. How often do you exercise? What kinds of exercise do you like?
   b. What kinds of exercise are popular in your country?

2. Work with other classmates. Talk about a sport or exercise you've always wanted to learn.

46. You're in great shape!

Karen and Dennis run into a friend while they're taking a walk.

A

Mike Hi, Dennis! Hi, Karen!

Dennis Mike! Hey, you've lost a lot of weight.

Mike Forty pounds.

Dennis No kidding! How much do you weigh now?

Mike Around 160 pounds.

Karen You're in great shape, Mike.

Mike Well, I get a lot of exercise.

Dennis I really ought to start doing something. I'm starting to get a potbelly.

B

Mike Do you ever get any exercise, Dennis?

Dennis Not regularly. I've always hated running.

Mike Well, why don't you do something else?

Dennis I enjoy biking. In fact, I used to go on long bike trips, but lately I can never seem to find the time.

Mike Well, here's your big chance. I'm biking to Lake Walden next weekend with some friends of mine. How about joining us, both of you?

Karen Sounds great!

Dennis Well, I was planning to work Saturday. . . .

Karen Oh, come on, Dennis. You can work some other time. Uh, do you know where I can rent a bike, Mike?

Mike There's a bicycle shop somewhere around here. Say, how tall are you?

Karen Five four.

Mike You're about the same height as my sister . . . or maybe an inch taller. She has two bikes. I'm sure you can borrow one of hers.

Dennis I didn't know you had a sister, Mike.
Mike I have a twin sister.
Dennis Really? Is she just like you?
Mike Oh no. She's very different from me. To tell the truth, we don't really have much in common, but we get along really well.
Dennis Did you use to get along when you were younger?
Mike Oh, yeah. We've always gotten along well.
Dennis You're lucky. My brother and I used to fight all the time.

Figure it out

1. Listen to the conversations. Then choose *a* or *b*.

1. a. Dennis probably hasn't seen Mike for a long time.
   b. Dennis probably sees Mike every week.
2. a. Dennis wants to start running, but can't find the time.
   b. Dennis doesn't get enough exercise.

2. Listen again and say *True, False,* or *It doesn't say.*

1. Mike used to weigh 200 pounds.
2. Dennis used to exercise more.
3. Dennis likes to run.
4. Dennis has been too busy to take long bike trips.
5. Karen doesn't have her own bike.
6. Mike's sister is going to Lake Walden next weekend too.
7. Mike's sister is a year older than he is.
8. Mike and his sister used to fight a lot.

3. Fill in the blanks with *to work* or *working*.

1. I enjoy *working*.
2. I was planning _____ .
3. I'm _____ tomorrow.
4. I used _____ harder.
5. How about _____ late?

47. I've always enjoyed swimming.

TALK ABOUT EXERCISE • TALK ABOUT LIKES AND DISLIKES • INFINITIVES VS. GERUNDS

 ► Listen to the conversation. Circle **W** for the things the woman likes to do in her free time. Circle **M** for the things the man likes to do.

W M   W M   W M   W M
1. play tennis   2. run   3. roller-skate   4. ice-skate

► Listen to the two possible conversations.
► Act out similar conversations with a partner. Use the activities in the pictures above or your own information.

A Do you like to swim?

B Yes, I've always enjoyed swimming. In fact, I've started swimming regularly.

B No, I've never liked swimming very much.

> I've always liked swimming.
> I've always enjoyed swimming.
> I've never liked swimming.
> I've always hated swimming.

► Study the frames: Infinitives vs. gerunds

I love	
I like	**to swim.**
I hate	**swimming.**
I've started	

| I enjoy | **swimming.** |
| I've stopped | |

Gerunds, such as *swimming*, are formed the same way as present participles, by adding -*ing*.

 ► Listen to the conversation.
► In groups of three, have similar conversations using the pictures below or your own information.

A I like to get up early on weekends.
B Me too. I like to get up early and enjoy the whole day.
C Not me! I hate getting up early on weekends.

I like to paint.   I like to play soccer.   I like to read.   I like to sleep late.

► Talk to your classmates. Find out what they like to do on the weekend. Find out what they hate to do. Report to the class.

Yong Hee and Carlos both like shopping.
Lee hates to clean the house.

6 ► **Listen to the conversation and practice it with a partner.**
► **Act out similar conversations, using your own information.**

A Do you ever get any exercise?
B I run five miles a day. How about you?
A Hardly ever. I ought to exercise more, but I can never seem to find the time.

ought to = should

Do you ever get any exercise?
I run five miles a day.
I play tennis every other day.
I work out three times a week.
Sometimes I roller-skate.
I go biking once in a while.
I used to swim, but I haven't lately.
Hardly ever.
I can never seem to find the time.

7 ► **Match the descriptions with the pictures.**
► **How much does each person weigh now?**

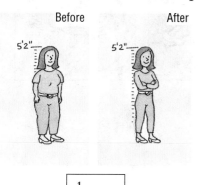

Before   After

1. ____

Before   After

2. ____

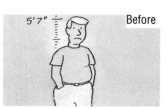

5'7"   Before

5'7"   After

5'7"   Later

3. ____

a. Fred used to weigh 180. He lost 40 pounds. Then he gained it all back!
b. Lucy lost 30 pounds. She used to weigh 140.
c. Dave gained 35 pounds. He used to weigh 135.

8 ► **Listen to the conversation.**
► **Act out similar conversations about the people in the pictures above or people you know.**

Has he lost weight?

A Your husband looks great. Has he lost weight?
B Yeah. Twenty pounds.
A That's great! What does he weigh now?
B 160 pounds.
A How tall is he?
B Five foot ten.

five foot ten = five feet ten inches (5'10")

Feet and inches	Meters
5'	1.52
5'2"	1.57
5'4"	1.63
5'6"	1.68
5'8"	1.73
5'10"	1.78
6'	1.83

1 pound (lb.) = 0.45 kilogram (kg)

1 kilogram = 2.2 pounds

1 meter (m) = 3.28 feet
1 foot (ft.) = 0.30 meter
1 inch (in.) = 2.54 centimeters (cm)

Pounds	Kilograms	Kilograms	Pounds
5	2.3	2	4.4
10	4.5	5	11
25	11.4	10	22
50	22.7	25	55
100	45.5	50	110

For more weights and measures, see p. 86.

48. I'm going biking with a friend of mine.

▶ **Listen to the two possible conversations and practice them with a partner.**

▶ **Act out similar conversations, using the activities in the pictures or your own information.**

A I'm going biking with Bill and a friend of ours on Saturday. How about joining us?

B Sounds great.   **B** Well, I was planning to work on Saturday.

Other ways to say it

Would you like to join us?
Do you want to come along?
Why don't you come with us?

▶ **Study the frame: Possessive pronouns and possessives of names**

a friend	of	mine
		yours
		his
		hers
		ours
		theirs
		John's

Some activities

go dancing   go camping   go skiing

ASK WHERE TO GET SOMETHING

▶ **Listen to the two possible conversations and practice them with a partner.**

A Do you know where I can rent a bike?

B There's a bicycle shop on Main Street. It's called Hot Wheels.

B Oh, I have one I never use. You can borrow mine.

rent a car
buy a newspaper
get a good haircut
make a phone call

▶ **Complete the conversations with questions, using the phrases in the box.**

▶ **Listen to check your work.**

▶ **Practice the conversations with a partner.**

? — Yeah, at the newsstand down the street.

1.

? — Sure. There's a public phone over there.

2.

▶ **Work with a partner. Ask three questions about where to get something in your city, town, or neighborhood. Your partner will answer.**

? — I know a great hairstylist, but he's expensive.

3.

? — There's a car rental place about a mile from here.

4.

49. Is your sister like you?

TALK ABOUT YOUR FAMILY • THE PAST WITH *USED TO*

1 ▶ **Listen to the two possible conversations and practice them with a partner.**
   ▶ **Act out similar conversations, using your own information.**

A Is your sister older than you or younger?
B She's five years older.
A Do you have a lot in common?

B Yes. We're a lot alike. We both enjoy doing things outdoors.

B Not really. Our interests are very different. (She likes . . .)

| Is your sister like you? Do you have a lot in common? | She's a lot like me. We're very similar. She's very different from me. | She's five years older. We're twins. She's two years younger. |

2 ▶ **Interview two classmates about their families. Report to the class.**

Marie has an older brother. Their interests are very different. She likes . . . but her brother enjoys . . .

3 ▶ **Listen to the two possible conversations and practice them with a partner.**
   ▶ **Act out similar conversations, using your own information.**

A Do you get along with your sister?
B Yes. Most of the time.
A Did you use to get along when you were younger?

B Yes. We've always gotten along well.

B Not too well. We used to fight a lot.

> Use *used to* to refer to something that took place repeatedly or over an extended period of time in the past:
>
> I **used to** take the bus to work.
> I **used to** live in Mexico.

4 ▶ **Study the frames: The past with *used to***

Where	**did** you		work?			**used to**	take the bus to work.
	Did you	**use to**	drive	to work?	I	**didn't use to**	drive to work, but I do now.
						never **used to**	drive to work, but I do now.

5 ▶ **Amy started a new job a few months ago. Complete her conversation with Jim. Use a form of *used to* and the verb in parentheses in each answer.**
   ▶ **Listen to check your work.**

Jim *What did you use to do* (do) before you came here?
Amy I was marketing director at Lowell and White.
Jim Oh, then you _____ (work) with Don Ford.
Amy Yes. As a matter of fact, we're good friends.
Jim _____ (travel) a lot for that job too?
Amy Hardly ever. That's something I love about this job. Of course I work harder now. I never _____ (work) late at the office on my old job.

50. A little exercise will do you good.

Doug is moving out of his apartment.

1

Ricky	Hey, what did you put in this box? It weighs a ton.
Doug	Oh, stop complaining. A little exercise will do you good.
Ricky	I get plenty of exercise already. I play basketball every day. In fact, I was planning to play today.
Doug	Well, we're almost finished. I guess I have more stuff than I thought. How about working, say, fifteen minutes more? Then we can order out for pizza. I'll treat.
Ricky	Sounds great. I'm so hungry I could eat a horse.
Sarah	Where do you want me to put this, Doug?
Doug	Hey, isn't that too heavy for you, Sarah?
Sarah	This is nothing. I lift weights.
Doug	Well, here, let me help you anyway. (*Grunts*) This box is heavier than I thought.
Ricky	I guess a little exercise would do you good. Maybe you ought to lift weights like Sarah.
Doug	Maybe I should. I used to be a lot stronger.
Sarah	You mean when you were young?
Doug	Funny, I thought I still was.

2. Figure it out

Say *True, False,* or *It doesn't say.*

1. Ricky hardly ever gets any exercise.
2. Doug, Ricky, and Sarah started working more than an hour ago.
3. Doug, Ricky, and Sarah are going to order a pizza in fifteen minutes.
4. Doug is going to pay for the pizza.
5. Doug isn't as strong as he was when he was younger.

3. Listen in

Sarah and Doug continue their conversation. Read the questions below. Then listen to the conversation and answer the questions.

1. Who is Ruth?
2. How tall is Ruth?
3. What has Ruth always enjoyed doing?

51. Your turn

Fill out the questionnaire and find out how long you will live.

If you received a low score, remember that it's never too late to change. What changes do you think you should make in your life? Discuss your answers with a partner.

How Long Will You Live?

We don't know how long we will live, but we do know that certain factors can lengthen or shorten a person's life. Use the questionnaire below to calculate (approximately) how many years you will live.

START WITH THE NUMBER 75.   75

1. SEX:
If you are a man,	subtract 3	____
If you are a woman,	add 4	____

2. LIFESTYLE:
If you live in a big city (over 2 million),	-3	____
If you live in a small town (under 10,000),	+2	____
If you work at a desk,	-3	____
If your work requires physical activity,	+3	____
If you exercise a lot (5 times a week for 30 minutes),	+2	____
If you live with someone,	+5	____
If you live alone,	-1	____

3. PERSONALITY:
If you sleep more than 10 hours a night,	-4	____
If you sleep less than 5 hours a night,	-4	____
If you are impatient,	-3	____
If you are easygoing,	+3	____
If you are happy,	+1	____
If you are unhappy,	-2	____

4. SUCCESS:
If you earn over $50,000 a year,	-2	____
If you finished college,	+1	____
If you have more than one college degree	+2	____
If you are 65 years old and still working,	+3	____

5. FAMILY BACKGROUND:
If any of your grandparents lived to 85,	+2	____
If all four of your grandparents lived to 80,	+6	____
If either of your parents died of a heart attack before 50,	-4	____
If any parent, brother, or sister has heart disease or diabetes,	-3	____

6. HEALTH:
If you smoke more than 2 packs of cigarettes a day,	-8	____
If you smoke more than half a pack of cigarettes a day,	-3	____
If you are overweight by 50 pounds,	-8	____
30 pounds,	-3	____
15 pounds,	-2	____
If you have a medical exam every year,	+2	____

7. AGE ADJUSTMENT:
If you are 30-40,	+2	____
40-50,	+3	____
50-70,	+4	____
If you are over 70,	+5	____

YOU WILL LIVE APPROXIMATELY_____YEARS.

How to say it

Practice the phrases.
Then practice the conversation.

some friends of Bill's
　　　　　　　[z]

a cousin of Lois's
　　　　　　[ɪz]

a friend of Pat's
　　　　　[s]

A I'm going skiing with Pat and some friends of Bill's on Saturday. One of them is a cousin of Lois's.

B Really? A friend of Pat's called me last night and invited me too. But I don't ski.

52.

Have you ever taken a long flight? Do you ever exercise in your seat when you fly? Look at the pictures in the article. Do you think these exercises would be helpful on a long flight?

The human body is made to move and it works best when it gets regular exercise. These days, however, we spend a lot of time sitting down—in an office chair, at the theater, or in a comfortable airline seat—where there is very little freedom of movement. Here is an exercise program that will help keep you comfortable on long trips so that you arrive refreshed and relaxed.

1. Jogging on the spot.
A warm-up exercise.
Lift your heels as high as possible, one foot at a time. At the same time, lift your arms in a bent position and move forward and backward as if you were walking. Continue for 1–3 minutes.

2. Shoulder rolling.
For shoulder joints and muscles.
Move your shoulders gently in large circles in both forward and backward directions. Repeat 6 times in each direction.

3. Forward bending with stomach in.
For your stomach muscles.
Pull in your stomach. Bend forward while lifting your toes high. Put your toes back on the floor, relax your stomach, and sit up again. Repeat 30 times.

4. Head turning and nodding.
For your neck and spine.
Turn your head all the way to the right. Nod a few times. Do the same to the left. Repeat 6 times on each side.

5. Hand turning.
For your wrists.
Turn your hands over and open your fingers. Return your hands to their first position and relax them. Repeat 15 times.

6. Knees and elbows.
For blood circulation.
Raise your right knee to your left elbow. Then raise your left knee to your right elbow. Repeat 10 times.

1. Read the article. Then match the parts of the body with the words below.

a. heel
b. elbow
c. neck
d. toes
e. fingers
f. stomach
g. shoulder
h. head
i. hand
j. foot
k. arm
l. knee

2. Practice doing each exercise.

1. Which exercise is the easiest for you?
2. Which exercise is the hardest for you?

Review of units 5-7

1 ▶ Use the map to figure out a question to complete each conversation.
Then combine each pair of sentences in brackets [ ], using *when*, *until*,
or *as soon as*.

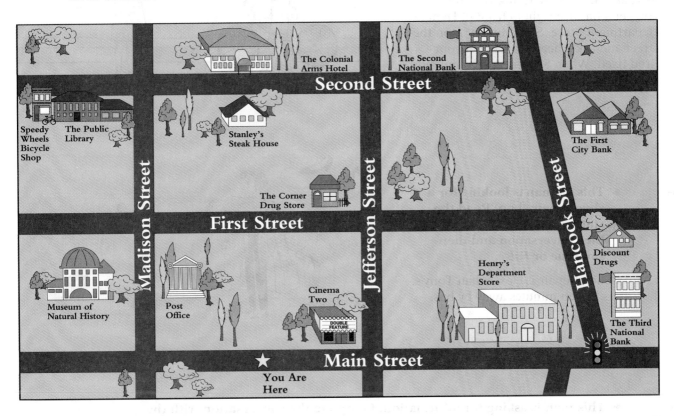

1. **A** *How do I get to Discount Drugs?*
   B Go straight ahead on Main.
   [You'll pass a big department store. Turn left.]
   as soon as
   As soon as you pass a big department store,
   turn left.
   It'll be on your right near the end of the block.

2. **A** _____?
   B It's on Madison Street.
   [Go to the corner. Then turn right.] *when*
   That's Madison.
   [Then go straight ahead. You'll come to a post
   office.] *until*
   It's right across the street from the post office.

3. **A** _____?
   B There's one about three blocks from here.
   [Walk to the corner. Then turn left on
   Jefferson.] *when*
   [Stay on Jefferson. You'll get to Second
   Street.] *until*
   Turn left. It'll be on your right, about halfway
   down the block.

4. **A** _____?
   B Yes, it's the next street after Jefferson.
   [Just stay on Main. You'll come to a traffic
   light.] *until*
   There'll be a big department store on your
   left. You can't miss it.

2A ▶ **Student A follows the
instructions below.
Student B follows the
instructions on page 78.**

Student A: You're walking along the
street in front of Henry's Department
Store. Student B stops you on the street
and asks for information. Use the map
to answer Student B's questions.

2B ▶ **Student B follows the instructions below. Student A follows the instuctions on page 77.**

Student B: You're riding your bike and you get a flat tire right in front of Henry's Department Store. Stop Student A on the street and ask where you can get your tired fixed. When Student A recommends a place, ask how to get there.

3 ▶ **This woman is looking for a shoe repair shop. Read the statements below. Listen to the conversation and then say *True* or *False*.**

1. Ed's Shoe Repair is closer than Tony's.
2. Ed's is fifteen minutes away by bus.

4 ▶ **This man is asking for information. Complete the conversation with the comparative or superlative form of the adjectives in parentheses.**
▶ **Listen to check your work.**

A I'm looking for a place to stay. Could you recommend a good hotel?

B Well, The Colonial Arms is *the nicest* (nice) hotel in town, but it's also _____ (expensive). Rooms start at $200 a night.

A Oh! Is there anything _____ (expensive)?

B Let me see. The Windsor is a lot _____ (reasonable), but it's _____ (far) away. You'll have to take a taxi to get there.

A O.K., but I need to get some cash. Is there a bank with a 24-hour cash machine near here?

B Actually, there are three—the Third National, the Second National, and the First City.

A Which one is _____ (easy) to get to?

B Well, the Third National is _____ (close) than the other two. It's only about two blocks from here.

A Thank you. You've been very helpful.

B You're welcome.

5 ▸ Nick calls his friend Wendy at her office and leaves a message for her. Put the conversation in order.
▸ Listen to check your work.

___ I'll give her the message as soon as she gets back.
___ Yes, please. This is Nick Damato. Would you please ask her to call me? My number is 555-3929.
___ She should be back by two. Would you like to leave a message?
___ Can I speak to Wendy Jacobs, please?
___ When do you expect her back?
_1_ Good afternoon, Rockwell and Stone.
___ Thank you.
___ I'm sorry, but she's not in the office right now.

6 ▸ Work with a partner. Play these roles.

Student A: Call a friend's office and ask the receptionist (Student B) if you can speak to your friend. If your friend is not there, leave a message.

Student B: Play the role of the receptionist. Student A calls and wants to speak to someone who's not in the office now. Offer to take a message. Complete the message form.

7 ▸ Listen to the first part of each conversation and choose the best response.

1. a. Well, the most expensive one I can think of is Alfredo's.
   b. Well, the closest one I can think of is Alfredo's.

2. a. No, I'm afraid I don't.
   b. No, that place is too far.

3. a. It's faster by bus.
   b. It's about a ten-minute walk.

4. a. Oh, I'll get one for you.
   b. I'd be glad to.

5. a. May I tell him who's calling?
   b. I'll give him the message.

6. a. Oh, I'll copy them for you.
   b. Oh, I'll copy it for you.

7. a. Me too. I enjoy getting up early.
   b. Not me. I like to get up early.

8. a. Sure. There's a coffee shop just down the street.
   b. Sure. There's one on Main Street.

9. a. O.K. Sounds like fun.
   b. O.K. I've never liked dancing.

10. a. No, I can't seem to find the time.
    b. Yes, I used to play tennis.

► **Martha White just celebrated her one hundredth birthday. Read the interview about her life and about "the old days."**

MARTHA WHITE:
Clinton's Oldest Citizen

Mrs. White, have you always lived in Clinton?

All my life. As a matter of fact, I was born in this house. That's the way it used to be in the old days. People never used to move away from their home town. You were born in a place, and you lived there until you died.

Your first husband died ten years ago...

Yes, at the age of ninety-two. We had seventy wonderful years together. We were very much alike. Both of us loved a good conversation. People used to talk to each other more in the old days. Now they watch television.

Mrs. White, you've already lived a hundred years and you look as if you might live another hundred years. What's your secret?

Well, I laugh a lot. That's very important.

And I keep busy. I get a lot of exercise too. I've always enjoyed sports. I went skiing and horseback riding regularly until I was eighty-five. And I've always liked swimming. In fact, I still swim every day at the high school pool, and I've started running a little with my second husband.

When did you remarry?

Six years ago. I was ninety-four and he was a young man of eighty. A lot of people say I robbed the cradle!

Mrs. White, you're a hundred years old now. How do you feel?

Great! Not a day over ninety!

► **Talk about two things that used to be different in the old days, according to Mrs. White.**

► **How have things changed since you, your parents, or your grandparents were children? Make statements with *used to*, *didn't use to*, *never used to*, and *not ... anymore*.**

People didn't use to work on computers.
People used to use manual typewriters.

► **Work with a partner. Compare yourself to a family member. Are you alike or different? Be as specific as you can.**

I'm a lot like my father. We both like... We both enjoy...

► **Imagine you're celebrating your one hundredth birthday. Write a short article about yourself, telling about the things you've always liked to do, things you've never enjoyed doing, things you used to do, and things you never used to do. Before starting to write, follow the steps below.**

1. Make a list of things you've always liked to do.
2. Make a list of things you've never enjoyed doing.
3. Make a list of things you used to do, but don't do anymore.
4. Make a list of things that you never used to do, but that you've started doing.

VOCABULARY LIST

This list includes both productive and receptive words introduced in Student Book 3A. Productive words are those which students use actively in interaction exercises. Receptive words are those which appear only in opening conversations, comprehension dialogues, readings, and instructions, and which students need only understand. The following abbreviations are used to identify words: V = verb, N = noun, ADJ = adjective, ADV = adverb, CONJ = conjunction, PR = pronoun, R = receptive. Page numbers indicate the first appearance of a word.

A

a bit of 54
accent 34
accompany (V) 56 R
accomplishment 66 R
achievement 66 R
accuracy 37 R
act (N) 56 R
adjustment 75 R
administrative 58 R
adolescent 20
advancement 22 R
advantage 22 R
agency (advertising
  agency) 4
album 26
alike 73
all over 39
all set 7
allow (V) 26 R
along the way 12 R
aloud 66 R
alternate (V) 56 R
ambition 21 R
amount 42 R
amusement (park) 11 R
ancestor 42 R
announce (V) 39
anthropology 29
anymore 15
appetizer 44
archeologist 42 R
artifact 42 R
as a matter of fact 3
as if 76 R
asleep 39
assume (V) 56 R
assure (V) 19 R
at first sight 38 R
athletics 20
atmosphere 50
attract (V) 11 R
autobiographical 32 R
avoid (V) 56 R
aware 56 R
awfully 19 R

B

backward 76 R
bake (V) 62 R
bakery 51
barber 22 R
based (on) 29
basket 56 R
bathroom scale 54 R

be off to 2
be up to 10
become (V) 22 R
beginning (N) 14
behave (V) 56 R
behavior 56 R
bend (V) 76 R
benefit(s) 65 R
bent (ADJ) 76 R
best 24
big 10
bike (V) 68
birth (place of birth) 32 R
bite (a bite to eat) 40 R
blind 26 R
blood 30
blue-collar 22 R
board (V) 2
body of water 42 R
bone 42 R
boost (N) (=increase)
  66 R
borrow (V) 61
box office 27 R
bridge 6 R
brilliance 66 R
brilliant 31 R
brochure 5
build (V) 62 R
Bullet Train 28

C

cable car 6 R
calculate (V) 75 R
call (N) 10
cameo (appearance) 32 R
camp 20
camper 20
campfire 42 R
carbon 42 R
carry (V) 7
cash machine 78
castle 12 R
casual 66 R
catch (V) 2
cave (N) 42 R
centimeter 71 R
chance (N)
  (=opportunity) 20
channel (on TV) 26 R
charcoal 42 R
child 15
chocolate 64
chopstick 56 R
church 53
cigarette 75 R

cinema 31 R
circulation 76 R
circus 27
citizen 33 R
clean (V) 50
close (ADJ) 47
coast 11 R
combine (V) 11R
come across as 66 R
come over 10
comment (V) 19 R
commit (V) 31 R
common sense 21 R
complain (V) 74
comprehension 37 R
cone (ice cream cone) 39
confuse (V) 56 R
construction 18
consultant 66 R
contribute (V) 66 R
contribution 66 R
control (N) 67 R
controversy 42 R
copy (V) 79
corporate 66 R
cough (V) 2 R
counseling 20
counselor (guidance
  counselor) 20
count on 58
count out 56 R
coworker 64 R
cradle 80 R
creative 47
crime 31 R
crucial 66 R
culture 56 R
custom 12 R

D

dad (=father) 64
dance (N) 27
dancing (go dancing) 24
deal with 12 R
death 56 R
decide (V) 25
decision 40
decrease (V) 22 R
defend (V) 42 R
degree (college degree)
  75 R
deliver (V) 66 R
deny (V) 66 R
depart (V) 4 R
descendant 33 R
deserve (V) 66 R

desire (N) 11 R
destroy (V) 42 R
diabetes 75 R
die (V) 35
differ (from) 56 R
dig (N) 42 R
dine (out) 56 R
directly 42 R
director (marketing
  director) 73
disagreement 42 R
disappear (V) 66 R
discover (V) 42 R
discovery 42 R
district 6 R
distribute (V) 60
disturb (V) 31 R
diversity 33 R
do a favor 58
doubt (N) 42 R
down 3
drip (V) 39
dune (sand dune) 12 R
dwelling 42 R

E

edge 31 R
elsewhere 66 R
ending (N) 3
engineering 9 R
equipment 9 R
essential 66 R
estimate (V) 42 R
ethnic 33 R
evaluate (V) 37 R
everywhere 62
evidence 22 R
excited (about) 5
exhibit (N) 27
exotic 47
expect (V) 59
explain (V) 59
explore (V) 12 R
extended (ADJ) 73 R
extremely 21 R

F

fabulous 6 R
fall asleep 39
fan 11 R
fantasy 13 R
far 47
fashion (=way, manner)
  56 R

SUPPLEMENTARY VOCABULARY

IRREGULAR VERBS

Base form	Simple past	Past participle	Base form	Simple past	Past participle
be	was, were	been	lend	lent	lent
beat	beat	beaten	let	let	let
become	became	become	lie	lay	lain
begin	began	begun	lose	lost	lost
bend	bent	bent	make	made	made
bite	bit	bitten	mean	meant	meant
blow	blew	blown	meet	met	met
break	broke	broken	pay	paid	paid
bring	brought	brought	put	put	put
build	built	built	quit	quit	quit
buy	bought	bought	read	read [rɛd]	read [rɛd]
catch	caught	caught	ride	rode	ridden
choose	chose	chosen	ring	rang	rung
come	came	come	rise	rose	risen
cost	cost	cost	run	ran	run
cut	cut	cut	say	said	said
deal	dealt	dealt	see	saw	seen
dig	dug	dug	sell	sold	sold
do	did	done	send	sent	sent
draw	drew	drawn	set	set	set
drink	drank	drunk	shake	shook	shaken
drive	drove	driven	shoot	shot	shot
eat	ate	eaten	shut	shut	shut
fall	fell	fallen	sing	sang	sung
feed	fed	fed	sit	sat	sat
feel	felt	felt	sleep	slept	slept
fight	fought	fought	slide	slid	slid
find	found	found	speak	spoke	spoken
fit	fit	fit	spend	spent	spent
fly	flew	flown	stand	stood	stood
forget	forgot	forgotten	steal	stole	stolen
get	got	gotten	stick	stuck	stuck
give	gave	given	strike	struck	struck
go	went	gone	sweep	swept	swept
grow	grew	grown	swim	swam	swum
have	had	had	swing	swung	swung
hear	heard	heard	take	took	taken
hide	hid	hidden	teach	taught	taught
hit	hit	hit	tear	tore	torn
hold	held	held	tell	told	told
hurt	hurt	hurt	think	thought	thought
keep	kept	kept	throw	threw	thrown
know	knew	known	understand	understood	understood
lay	laid	laid	wear	wore	worn
lead	led	led	win	won	won
leave	left	left	write	wrote	written

WEIGHTS AND MEASURES

English System

Linear Measure

12 inches (in.)	=	1 foot (ft.)
3 feet	=	1 yard (yd.)
1760 yards	=	1 mile (mi.)
(5280 feet)		

Liquid Measure

16 fluid ounces (oz.)	=	1 pint (pt.)
2 pints	=	1 quart (qt.)
4 quarts	=	1 gallon (gal.)

Weight

16 ounces	=	1 pound (lb.)
1 ton	=	2000 pounds (U.S.)
	=	2240 pounds (Great Britain)

Metric and English Equivalents

Linear Measure

1 inch (in.)	=	2.54 centimeters (cm)
1 foot	=	30.48 centimeters
1 yard	=	0.9144 meters (m)
1 mile	=	1609.3 meters

Liquid Measure

1 quart	=	0.946 liters
1 gallon	=	13.78 liters

Weight

1 ounce	=	28.3 grams (g)
1 pound	=	0.45 kilograms (kg)
1 ton (U.S.)	=	907.18 kilograms
1 ton (Great Britain)	=	1016 kilograms

HOW TO READ LARGE NUMBERS

Money	Street addresses	Telephone numbers
$1,003: a/one thousand (and) three dollars	1003 Moore Street: ten-oh-three Moore Street	555-1003: five-five-five—one-oh-oh-three
$1,035: a/one thousand (and) thirty-five dollars	1035 Moore Street: ten–thirty-five Moore Street	555-1035: five-five-five—one-oh-three-five
$1,500: fifteen hundred dollars or a/one thousand five hundred dollars	1500 Moore Street: fifteen hundred Moore Street	555-1500: five-five-five—one-five hundred or five-five-five—one-five-oh-oh
$1,853: a/one thousand eight hundred (and) fifty-three dollars	1853 Moore Street: eighteen–fifty-three Moore Street	555-1853: five-five-five—one-eight-five-three
$3,200: thirty-two hundred dollars or three thousand two hundred dollars	3200 Moore Street: thirty-two hundred Moore Street	555-3200: five-five-five—three-two hundred or five-five-five—three-two-oh-oh
$4,253: four thousand two hundred (and) fifty-three dollars	4253 Moore Street: forty-two–fifty-three Moore Street	555-4253: five-five-five—four-two-five-three
$10,902: ten thousand nine hundred (and) two dollars	10902 Moore Street: ten–nine-oh-two Moore Street	
$21,500: twenty-one thousand five hundred dollars	21500 Moore Street: twenty-one–five hundred Moore Street	

Calendar years are read the same way as street addresses.

PRONUNCIATION

STRESS AND INTONATION

Affirmative statement: Nice to meet you.

Yes-no question: Are you going to go home now?

Information question: What do you think of these chairs?

The numbers above and below the intonation lines indicate the pitch: 1 is for the lowest level and 3 is for the highest.

PHONETIC SYMBOLS*

Consonants

[p]	pen, apple
[b]	bank, cabbage
[f]	far, after
[v]	very, have
[k]	coffee, like
[g]	good, again
[l]	letter, mile
[m]	many, name
[n]	never, money
[ŋ]	ring, sing
[w]	water, away
[θ]	think, with
[ð]	the, mother
[s]	some, dress
[z]	zero, busy
[ʃ]	shoe, information
[ʒ]	pleasure, measure
[tʃ]	children, teach
[dʒ]	job, age
[r]	right, hurry
[y]	year, million
[h]	he, hat, who
[t]	ten, can't
[d]	dinner, idea

Vowels

[I]	in, visit
[i]	meet, tea
[ɛ]	end, let, any
[æ]	ask, family
[a]	father, hot
[ɔ]	water, long
[ʊ]	could, put
[u]	you, room
[ə]	across, but
[ər]	her, work
[e]	wait, great
[o]	home, go
[aI]	dime, night
[ɔI]	toy, boy
[aʊ]	found, house

*[ə] and [ər] are used in this book, for both stressed and unstressed syllables. [y] is used instead of the International Phonetic Alphabet (IPA) [j].

ACKNOWLEDGMENTS

ILLUSTRATIONS

Storyline illustrations by Anna Veltfort: pages 2, 3, 10, 16, 17, 20, 30, 40, 54, 64, 74; 28 (bottom right), 76 (bottom), and 78 (middle right); pages 34, 39 (top), 70 (top), 72 (top), 78 (bottom), 79, and 80 (bottom) by Anne Burgess; pages 14, 15, 43, 44, 45, 46 (top right), and 73 (bottom right) by Hugh Harrison; pages 9, 16, 17,18, 66 (bottom), 68, and 69 by Randy Jones ; pages 7, 26, 27, 36, 37, 39 (bottom right), 46 (middle left and right), 50, 57, 58, 59, 62, 70, 71 (bottom right), 72 (bottom), and 73 by Gene Myers; pages 4, 5, 8, 61, 63 by Chris Reed; pages 1, 19, 48, 51, 53, 60, 71 (top left, middle, and right), 77, and 78 (top right) by Arnie Ten ; page 76 by Jan Watkins.

PHOTOS

Page 5 (top left) by Shinichi Kanno/FPG International; pages 5 (top middle) and 6 (top right) by Will & Deni McIntyre/Will McIntyre/Photo Researchers; page 5 (top right) by Art Stein/Photo Researchers; page 6 (first left) by L. Grant/FPG International; pages 6 (second left), 6 (fourth left), and 6 (fourth right) by Travelpix/FPG International; page 6 (second right), 56 (top right), 65 (top middle) by Comstock; page 6 (third left) by Bill Bachman/Photo Researchers; page 6 (third right) by Dale E. Boyer/Photo Researchers; page 11 (top right) by Haroldo and Flavia de Faria Castro/FPG International; page 11 (top left) by Stan Osolinski/FPG International; page 11 (middle right) by Mark Anderson/Camera Press London/Globe Photos; page 11 (bottom left) by Thomas Craig/FPG International; page 11 (bottom right), 28 (top middle), and 38 (bottom) by Superstock; page 12 (top left) by Rob Lang/FPG International; page 12 (bottom right) by Doug Plummer/Photo Researchers; page 13 (bottom left) by Rob Goldman/ FPG International; page 13 (bottom middle) by John T. Turner/FPG International; pages 13 (bottom right), and 22 (second) by Michael Krasowitz/FPG International; page 18 (first left) by Four by Five; page 18 (first right) by FPG International; page 18 (bottom left) by Chester Higgins, Jr./Photo Researchers; page 18 (bottom right) by M.B. Duda/ Photo Researchers; page 21 (top) and (middle) by Richard Hutchings/Photo Researchers; page 21 (bottom) by Ed Hoy/FPG International; page 22 (first) by Jeff Kaufman/FPG International; page 22 (third) by United Nations; page 22 (fourth) by Dick Luria/FPG International; page 23 (bottom left) by Adam Scull/Globe Photos; pages 23 (bottom right), 24 (top right), bottom right), 25 (top right), 63 (bottom left), (bottom middle), (bottom right) by Frank Labua; page 28 (top left) by Ch. Petit/Agence Vandystadt/ Photo Researchers; pages 28 (top right) and 29 (top left) by Paolo Koch/Photo Researchers; page 28 (bottom left) by Adam Hart-Davis/Science Photo Library/ Photo Researchers; page 28 (bottom middle) by Dave Bartruff/FPG International; page 28 (bottom right) by Hiroshi Harada/Dunq/Photo Researchers; page 29 (top right) by Victor Englebert/Photo Researchers; page 29 (bottom right) by Suzanne Murphy/FPG International; pages 31 (top right), (middle left), (middle right), (bottom left) by Photofest; pages 33 and 41 courtesy of Joan Karis; page 35 (top) from the collection of L. Milton Warshawsky/Culver Pictures; page 48 (top right and bottom right), and 49 (top left) by Roberto Lessia; page 55 (bottom right) by Steve Vidler/ Leo de Wys; page 56 (bottom right) by Tim Holt/Photo Researchers; page 63 (top left) by Daniel Quat/FPG International; page 63 (top right) by Raul Rubiera/FPG International; page 63 (bottom left), 65 (top right) by Tom Tracy/The Stock Shop; page 63 (bottom right) by Gary Buss/FPG International; page 65 (top left) by David Frazier/Photo Researchers; page 65 (bottom left) by Eunice Harris/Photo Researchers; page 65 (bottom middle) by Margaret Miller/Photo Researchers; page 65 (bottom right) by Ray Malace/FPG International; page 67 (top right) by Lok, Inc./FPG International; page 67 by Frederick McKinney/FPG International; page 73 (top right) by Porterfield-Chickering/Photo Researchers; page 73 (bottom right) by Charles Mayer/Photo Researchers; page 80 (top left) by Ron Chapple; page 80 (middle left) by Culver Pictures; page 80 (middle right) by Jose Luis Banus/FPG International.

REALIA

Pages 6, 12, 13, 16, 19, 21, 22, 23, 26, 27, 28, 29, 31, 32, 33, 37, 38, 41, 42, 47, 48, 50, 52, 53, 55, 56, 60, 66, 67, 75, 76, 77, and 80 by Siren Design.

REVIEWERS AND CONSULTANTS

For the preparation of the new edition, Regents/Prentice Hall would like to thank the following long-time users of Spectrum, whose insights and suggestions have helped to shape the content and format of the new edition: Motofumi Aramaki, Sony Language Laboratory, Tokyo, Japan; Associacão Cultural Brasil-Estados Unidos (ACBEU), Salvador-Bahia, Brazil; AUA Language Center, Bangkok, Thailand, Thomas J. Kral and faculty; Pedro I. Cohen, Professor Emeritus of English, Linguistics, and Education, Universidad de Panamá; ELSI Taiwan Language Schools, Taipei, Taiwan, Kenneth Hou and faculty; James Hale, Sundai ELS, Tokyo, Japan; Impact, Santiago, Chile; Instituto Brasil-Estados Unidos (IBEU), Rio de Janeiro, Brazil; Instituto Brasil-Estados Unidos No Ceará (IBEU-CE), Fortaleza, Brazil; Instituto Chileno Norteamericano de Cultura, Santiago, Chile; Instituto Cultural Argentino Norteamericano (ICANA), Buenos Aires, Argentina; Christopher M. Knott, Chris English Masters Schools, Kyoto, Japan; The Language Training and Testing Center, Taipei, Taiwan, Anthony Y. T. Wu and faculty; Lutheran Language Institute, Tokyo, Japan; Network Cultura, Ensino e Livraria Ltda, São Paulo, Brazil; Seven Language and Culture, São Paulo, Brazil.

PERMISSIONS

"Know What You're Worth Before You Seek a Raise", (p. 66). Reprinted by permission of Cynthia Hanson. First Appeared in *Chicago Tribune*, WOMANEWS.